React·Interact

SITUATIONS *for* COMMUNICATION

THIRD EDITION

Donald R. H. Byrd
Isis C. Clemente

longman.com

React Interact: Situations for Communication, Third Edition

Pearson Education, 10 Bank Street, White Plains, NY 10606

Vice president, director of publishing: Allen Ascher
Editorial director: Louisa Hellegers
Acquisitions editor: Eleanor Barnes
Senior development manager: Penny Laporte
Development editor: Stacey Hunter, Jill Kinkade
Vice president, director of design and production: Rhea Banker
Director of electronic production: Aliza Greenblatt
Executive managing editor: Linda Moser
Production manager: Ray Keating
Senior production editor: Sandra Pike
Production editor: Kathleen Silloway
Senior manufacturing buyer: Edith Pullman
Photo research: Frank Scalise
Cover design: Tracey Cataldo
Cover photo: © 2001 Dan Yaccarino/Stock Illustration Source
Text design: Patrice Sheridan
Text composition: Carlisle
Text art: Sandy Nichols
Front matter design: Wendy Wolf
Photo credits: See page xv.

Library of Congress Cataloging-in-Publication Data

Byrd, Donald R. H.
    React interact: situations for communication / Donald R. H. Byrd, Isis C. Clemente.—
3rd ed.
      p. cm.
    ISBN 0-13-022057-4
    1. English language—Textbooks for foreign speakers. 2. Communication—Problems,
exercises, etc. I. Clemente, Isis C. II. Title

PE1128 .B867 2001
428.3′4—dc21
                                   2001029336

7 8 9 10—BB—06

Contents

Section 6: SOCIAL PROBLEMS

Section 7: RELATIONSHIPS

To the Teacher

Welcome to the third edition of *React Interact*. Years of use by teachers and students have demonstrated that the success of *React Interact* is not a fad. This revision incorporates the invaluable feedback we have received from users of previous editions. Those who found the activities in earlier editions exciting and beneficial will not be disappointed. As with the previous editions, our goals are to: (1) improve students' communication skills in English through activities with engaging topics, themes, and ideas related to students and their interests; (2) increase students' knowledge of the English language; and (3) cherish the diversity of students' values while bringing an atmosphere of sharing and acceptance into the classroom. Meeting all three of these goals ensures that students build both communicative and linguistic competence—that is, fluency as well as accuracy in a supportive, sharing atmosphere.

React Interact brings together the three dimensions of natural communication: (1) content, (2) function, and (3) form. Content, the hook that captures the students' attention, is actually the carrier of function and form. Engaging content relates to the world, utilizes authentic discourse, and is comprehensible to different levels of students. In *React Interact*, rather than simplifying language samples, we have carefully looked for examples of simple, authentic language. Moreover, *React Interact* enables students to practice the six major functions of communication described by Van Ek (1975) and Wilkins (1976): (1) requesting and giving factual information; (2) expressing intellectual processes; (3) expressing emotion; (4) making moral judgments; (5) modifying people's behavior; and (6) interacting socially. These functions occur in isolation, or in combinations. *React Interact* implements these functional and formal linkages in each unit.

You will notice some changes in this edition. To make the content of *React Interact* more cohesive, the units have been grouped into themes such as "Life Choices" and "Relationships." The units are not arranged in order of difficulty; therefore, teachers can choose the units according to their students' interests and needs. Other changes include a greater variety of speaking activities and vocabulary exercises; writing activities that progress from guided to open-ended; pronunciation tasks; reading passages; and opinion surveys.

The twenty units in this book include various types of activities: discussing topics, summarizing, taking a survey, debating, solving a problem, answering questions, paraphrasing, filling in blanks, completing sentences, and matching exercises.

Each unit of *React Interact* has six sections: (1) Reaction (Introductory pictures with thought-provoking questions); (2) Interaction (individual and group communicative activities); (3) Opinion Survey (a survey and follow-up activity on the unit topic); (4) Reading Reaction (another slant on the unit topic); (5) Written Reaction (a vocabulary exercise and writing activities focused on the unit topic); and (6) Pronunciation (a quick, contextualized pronunciation activity gleaned from the language used in the unit).

When conducting these communication activities, it is important to treat students' opinions and feelings with understanding and sensitivity. The situations in this book deal with contemporary and sometimes controversial issues. They are not intended to offend anyone. Encourage your students to keep an open mind. However, if a situation seems to be "touchy," it is better to drop the discussion. Simply state that the purpose of conversation practice is to learn, not to offend. As the teacher, you are the best judge of which units will be successful with your group and which units you should not do at all. Don't be surprised if your choices vary with each class's personality and

Tips for Teaching *React Interact*

1. Adopt a feeling of acceptance for students' views.
2. Encourage students to share that same feeling of acceptance among themselves.
3. Listen to the students, and encourage them to listen to each other.
4. Avoid moralizing. No opinion is "right" or "wrong." Keep an open mind.
5. Be objective and fair. Don't take sides in an ongoing discussion.
6. Keep your opinions to yourself. (If students ask, you can tell them after their discussion is over.)
7. Use clarifying, supportive responses (e.g., "Do you mean . . . ?")
8. Encourage students to paraphrase rather than depend on the same "stock" phrases.
9. Use the vocabulary in the context of the topic under discussion.
10. Allow enough time for each activity.
11. For each activity, tell students what to do, how to do it, and how much time they have.
12. Vary the student dynamics (e.g., individual, pairs, small groups, etc.)
13. During discussions, focus on WHAT students are communicating, not so much on HOW.
14. Keep a record of students' persistent errors and address them afterwards.

taste. This flexibility makes the use of *React Interact* unique with each of your groups.

Most tasks should first be done individually. Then students can compare their responses. A variation is to divide the class into small groups and assign a different task from the Interaction activities to each group. Alternatively, assign the task to lead the small group discussion to a single student. Assign a student "secretary" to keep notes on the discussion, record troublesome vocabulary, summarize important arguments, and report that group's opinion to the entire class.

Some situations allow for a debate format. Divide the class into two sections representing the pro and con arguments. For a twist, ask the students who represented a *pro* argument to come up with a *con* argument and vice versa. Be sensitive to issues that might be too personal.

The tasks in Written Reaction, designed as follow-up activities, vary from guided writing practice to open-ended assignments. They echo the structure, vocabulary, and topics of the oral practice. They are best done as homework. Also included in Written Reaction is a treatment vocabulary, which can also be completed outside of class.

The inclusion of the Pronunciation section makes *React Interact* unique as a multiple-purpose conversation textbook. The pronunciation activities, rather than presenting the English sound segments as isolated words, treat the sound stretches that occur naturally in sentences. These activities are based on phrases that occur in the unit. It is important to model these sentences and phrases so that your students hear the target sound. You should not let the pronunciation tasks take up too much time. A good rule of thumb is to spend no more than ten minutes on the pronunciation activities.

The longer Interaction situations may be used over two class periods, allowing for distillation of students' ideas, opinions, and reactions during the time between the two class meetings. However, try to avoid having to stop class in the middle of an interesting discussion. Assign time limitations before students begin the activity. If you have opted to extend the unit beyond one class meeting, make students aware of your plans.

For the activities in *React Interact* to work effectively, teachers must at times, after the students are on task, fade into the wallpaper. This disappearing act is difficult for some teachers, but its benefit to students is clear. Students need to learn to function independently in English in order to develop strategic competence—the ability to use their language to learn more language.

We believe that *React Interact* will be a tool that will enhance communication among your students. It will give them the opportunity to express their feelings and opinions about a variety of engaging topics.

DONALD R. H. BYRD AND ISIS C. CLEMENTE

To the Student

You have your own ideas and opinions. Why don't you try to talk about them in English? This book, *React Interact*, will help you.

You can talk about yourself and your ideas. You can listen to other students talk about themselves and their ideas. You can compare ideas. You will not always agree with each other, but perhaps you will understand each other better. Also, you will probably understand your own feelings better. Maybe some of your opinions will change. Who knows? By discussing your ideas with others, you learn to express yourself in English.

There are many topics in this book—real-life topics such as love and marriage, emotions, work, occupations, and personal problems. Some topics are fantasy and can help you develop your imagination.

This book will also help you learn a lot of vocabulary. You can use these new words and expressions when you talk about your ideas with other students. In the Interaction section, you can first work by yourself and then talk about your ideas with other students. They can explain their ideas to you. The Opinion Survey contains many statements that will make you think. Other students' reactions will often be different from yours. These personal differences, of course, are typical of real life. You can understand another person's point of view even if you do not agree with that person.

You will learn to speak better, too. Study the pronunciation exercises. These exercises will help you say real phrases and sentences in English, not just isolated words. Furthermore, these exercises will help you understand native speakers when they speak fast. Then, you can practice your writing by doing the Written Reaction exercises at home. These exercises help you summarize the ideas in each unit. You can put your own thoughts in writing so that your writing is personal. You write about your own feelings.

For most exercises in *React Interact*, don't worry about "right" or "wrong" answers. Express your opinions and listen to the opinions of other students. Share your feelings with others, and they will share their feelings with you. Try to understand each other. You can learn from others, and others can learn from you.

You will learn from *React Interact* if you:

- think about the situation
- become familiar with the vocabulary
- express your ideas
- listen to the ideas of other students
- try to understand how other students feel
- explain someone else's ideas to another student
- re-examine your own ideas
- agree or disagree, if you like
- write down your ideas

With *React Interact*, you will learn more about yourself, other people, and the world around you. Your English will also improve. You will have fun, too! Good luck!

DONALD R. H. BYRD AND ISIS C. CLEMENTE

Acknowledgments

The success of *React Interact* continues to surprise us. It has touched so many people's lives—people who have expressed their gratitude for this textbook's respect for the humanity of learning English. After all, what unites us as humans more than our common gift of language? *React Interact* has been influential in students and teachers reaching a deeper understanding of each other and of their similarities and differences as human beings.

This third edition of *React Interact* did not come about easily. It has witnessed various publishing mergers over the years, and as a result, is likely to reach an even bigger population of people studying English. We are grateful to the many people at Prentice Hall and Pearson Education who helped to mother the revision of this edition: Sheryl Olinsky, a gifted and supportive editor who came up with a plan for revision; Louisa Hellegers, whose editorial reputation is well established and respected; Penny Laporte, whom we have known for years; and Eleanor Barnes, who kept us pretty much on schedule. Last, our sincere gratitude goes to our Development Editor, Jill Kinkade, who always gave us well-thought-out feedback, listened, suggested options, and showed a willingness to compromise. The extra work, the negotiating, and delays have all paid off. We can all be proud of the result.

A number of TESOL professionals, whether they know it or not, have helped to shape the philosophy that supports this book. In particular, we wish to acknowledge the work of four people: Gertrude Moskowitz, who was one of the first to understand the need for affective involvement in learning materials; Tracy Terrell, who spent hours with Donald discussing the affective influence in overall acquisition of language competence; Earl Stevick, whose *Helping People Learn English* was one of the first methods texts Donald was exposed to at Georgetown; and Mary Finocchiaro, a pioneering mentor from the early days.

On a personal level, we are grateful to our families and friends for their continued support and encouragement during the revision of this edition. Many of the reading selections derive from our own personal experiences, and for those experiences we are ever thankful to our families and loved ones. We wish to thank Karen Byrd Ferguson and Jerry Byrd, Athanassios Doumanidis, Effie Papatzikou Cochran, Alfred Chiodo, Angela Parrina, Stanley J. Zelinski, III, Ector Cabetas, and Lloyd B. Madansky. This book belongs to them as well.

DONALD R. H. BYRD AND ISIS C. CLEMENTE

Photo Credits

Unit One

Feelings

Reaction

Which feelings in the photos are good?
When do you have these feelings?

Interaction

A. Below is a list of different feelings. If you think the feeling is good, write a plus sign (+). If you think the feeling is bad, write a minus sign (–). Compare your answers.

_____ 1. anger   _____ 5. disappointment   _____ 8. fear

_____ 2. embarrassment _____ 6. nervousness   _____ 9. enthusiasm

_____ 3. pride   _____ 7. boredom   _____ 10. jealousy

_____ 4. love

B. Look at the photos on page 2. How does each person feel? With a partner, talk about the people. Use words from the box.

Example

He feels embarrassed.

They look angry.

afraid	embarrassed	proud	angry	nervous
loved	bored	enthusiastic	disappointed	jealous

C. Discuss these questions.

How do you feel when

1. you are in a theater with a lot of people, and someone shouts, "Fire!"?

2. you pass a very difficult test?

3. the boss's son gets your job?

4. you are in an elevator that stops between floors?

5. you are in the dentist's chair for the first time?

6. a good friend from far away telephones you?

7. you see your boyfriend or girlfriend with another person?

8. you have an opportunity to do something new and interesting?

Pronunciation — *-ed* and *-ing* Adjectives

The *–ed* ending sounds like [ɪd], [t], or [d]. The *–ing* ending sounds like [ɪŋ]. An *–ed* adjective describes a person's feeling. An *–ing* adjective describes the cause of the feeling.

❶ Listen to your teacher read this dialogue.

FRITZ: The math class isn't very exciting, is it?

JILL: No, it's boring. I was so bored yesterday I almost went to sleep. I was so embarrassed.

FRITZ: That's surprising. You were always interested in math.

JILL: Not anymore. I'm really disappointed in this class.

❷ Repeat the dialogue after your teacher.

❸ With a partner, practice the dialogue between Jill and Fritz.

D. Work in pairs.

1. Tell your partner about a situation that makes you feel good. Then ask if your partner feels the same way.

Example

STUDENT A: How do you feel when you're with good friends?

STUDENT B: I feel happy because they accept me the way I am. What about you?

STUDENT A: I feel loved because I am with people who care about me.

2. Tell your partner about a situation that makes you feel bad. Then ask if your partner feels the same way.

Example

STUDENT A: I feel nervous when I am in a crowd of strangers. Do you ever feel that way?

STUDENT B: Yes, especially when everyone is looking at me.

3. Tell your partner about ways you react to bad feelings. Then ask how your partner reacts to bad feelings.

Example

STUDENT A: When I feel afraid, I whistle a song. What do you do?

STUDENT B: I breathe deeply.

4. Tell your partner what you like to do when you have good feelings. Then ask what your partner likes to do.

Example

STUDENT A: I like to dance alone in my room when I feel happy. What about you?

STUDENT B: I like to invite all my friends to go out.

E. Work in groups.

1. Play the game "What is . . . ?" Sit in a circle and take turns. Ask and answer questions about the words in part A on page 3.

Example

STUDENT A: What is pride?

STUDENT B: Pride is doing well on a hard test.

STUDENT C: Pride is knowing my English has improved a lot.

STUDENT D: Pride is seeing my daughter graduate from college.

2. Talk about a time when you felt embarrassed.

Describe

1. what happened.

2. where you were.

3. what you felt.

4. why you felt that way.

5. what you will do if it happens again.

Opinion Survey: Feelings

A. Complete the survey. Circle *A* if you agree with the statements or *D* if you disagree with the statements. If you are not sure, circle *?*.

	A	D	?
1. Our feelings control us.	A	D	?
2. Some people are naturally happy and enthusiastic.	A	D	?
3. Some people are nervous by nature.	A	D	?
4. We sometimes get bored with necessary activities.	A	D	?
5. Enthusiastic people are not usually serious.	A	D	?
6. Logic is more important than feelings.	A	D	?
7. Sometimes anger is appropriate.	A	D	?
8. Jealousy is a part of love.	A	D	?
9. Everyone is afraid of something.	A	D	?
10. In order to be happy, you have to be rich.	A	D	?

B. Compare your answers with the other students in your class. Find out how many agree or disagree with the statements. Use numbers to report your class's opinions.

Example

Nine out of ten students agree that our feelings control us.

Reading Reaction

A. Why was this young person embarrassed? Read this story and find out.

An Embarrassing Situation

Do you remember when you were twelve years old? It was a confusing time for me. When I was twelve, I had a very embarrassing situation. I went to the family barber, Mr. Willard, and he cut my hair very short. All my friends had long hair back then. That was the style. Mr. Willard didn't care much for style. I didn't want to be different, and I looked like a plucked chicken. I even missed a few days of school because of my embarrassment. My sister was amused. She told me not to be so disappointed. After all, she said, the hair will grow back. Still, to me it was very upsetting.

I learned a valuable lesson from this situation. Today when I go to the barber, I always say exactly how I want my hair. I advise you

(continued)

to do the same. Speak to the barber before you sit down in that revolving chair. Explain exactly what you want. Watch carefully in the mirror as the barber cuts your hair. Don't be frightened to speak up. Barbers want their customers to be happy. They welcome your instructions.

I was probably too sensitive about my hair then. Now, at my age, I'm just proud of the hair that I have. By the way, Mr. Willard no longer cuts my hair. He's retired. His daughter Wilhelmina, a hairstylist, runs the shop. She not only cuts my hair, but she also styles the hair of my wife and children. No more plucked chickens.

B. Based on the reading, circle the words that best complete the sentences.

1. The writer is a (child / man / woman / barber).

2. The writer's sister was (happy / confused / amused / proud).

3. The young boy was (proud of / embarrassed by / confused by / amused by) the haircut.

4. The writer is now (a hairstylist / confused / embarrassed / married).

5. The writer advises the reader to (tell the barber what you want / cut your own hair / go to a hairstylist / go to another barber).

6. Wilhelmina is *not* (a shopkeeper / Mr. Willard's daughter / the writer's hairstylist / the writer's wife).

C. Answer these questions with a partner.

1. What happened to the writer when he was twelve?
2. How is the writer different now?
3. How is Mr. Willard different now?
4. What advice does the writer give?

Written Reaction

A. Match the adjectives with their opposites.

_c_	1. afraid	a. ashamed
____	2. enthusiastic	b. hated
____	3. happy	c. brave
____	4. angry	d. calm
____	5. proud	e. disinterested
____	6. bored	f. pleased
____	7. loved	g. sad
____	8. nervous	h. excited

B. Write four sentences about different situations that make you feel happy, proud, enthusiastic, or loved.

Example

I feel happy when I go to the beach.

1. _____
2. _____
3. _____
4. _____

C. Write four sentences about situations that make you feel afraid, angry, jealous, or nervous.

Example

I feel nervous when I meet new people.

1. _____
2. _____
3. _____
4. _____

D. Write about a situation that was embarrassing. Give your writing a title. Describe what happened, how you felt, why you felt that way, and what you will do if it happens again. Give some advice for a friend in the same situation. Look back at the reading on pages 5–6 as an example.

Unit Two

Picture Gallery

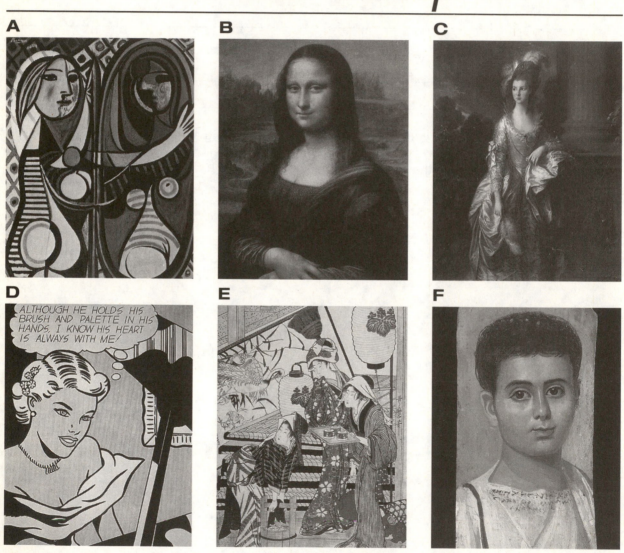

A

B

C

D

E

F

Reaction

How are these paintings similar? How are they different?
Which one is your favorite? Why?

Interaction

A. Match the following descriptions with the paintings on page 8. Discuss your answers in a group.

1. a geometric interpretation of the person   __A__
2. a comic book style of contemporary art   _____
3. a Japanese print   _____
4. an 18th-century person of elegance and fashion   _____
5. a Renaissance portrait of a smiling and mysterious woman   _____
6. an ancient Greek portrait from Egypt   _____

B. Everyone has different feelings about art. With a partner, ask and answer questions about the paintings.

Example

STUDENT A: Which painting is the most realistic?

STUDENT B: I think painting B is the most realistic.

Which portrait is

1. the most realistic?	6. the most abstract?
2. the most valuable?	7. the most famous?
3. the most detailed?	8. the newest?
4. the oldest?	9. the most interesting?
5. the saddest?	10. the strangest?

C. In a group, play Twenty Questions. Student A, choose a painting. The other students in your group will ask *yes/no* questions to discover the painting you chose. When one of the other students knows which painting you chose, that student will say which one it is. Then another student will choose a painting.

Example

STUDENT A: I'm thinking of a portrait. Which one is it?

STUDENT B: Is there a woman in the portrait?

STUDENT A: No, there isn't.

STUDENT C: Is it the oldest?

STUDENT A: No, it isn't.

STUDENT D: Is it from Europe?

STUDENT A: Yes, it is.

See page xv for full credit information about the paintings on page 8.

Pronunciation Superlatives

In rapid speech, the pronunciation of *the* and *most* in superlative adjectives changes. Notice the changes in the following cases:

- Before a consonant, the *t* in *most* is silent: (the mos famous)
- Before a vowel, the *t* in *most* is pronounced: (the most abstract)
- Before a consonant, the *e* in *the* sounds like *uh*: (the newest)
- Before a vowel, the *e* in *the* sounds like *ee*: (the oldest)

1 Listen to your teacher read this dialogue.

INTERVIEWER: Tell us about your most recent work, Madame.

FRAULA: The newest work is this sculpture here, but as you see, it's not the most abstract.

INTERVIEWER: Is it the most expensive?

FRAULA: I don't discuss those things. Let's just say this: It's my best work.

2 Repeat the dialogue after your teacher.

3 With a partner, practice the dialogue between Fraula and the interviewer.

D. Discuss these questions.

1. How are artists important in society?
2. What sort of person is a good artist?
3. Why are most famous artists men?
4. Who are some famous female artists?
5. Besides painting, what are some other kinds of art?
6. How is art different from culture to culture?
7. How is modern art different from classical art?
8. What is a government's role regarding art?

E. Imagine that the paintings on page 8 are in one museum. With a partner, decide what to do in the following situations. Compare your answers with other pairs of students. Try to agree on one decision for each situation.

1. You are on the committee of the museum. You need to raise money. Which painting will you sell to get the most money?
2. A committee from another museum wants to buy a famous painting. Which painting will they buy from your museum?
3. One of the paintings is missing from the museum. Which one do you think is missing?
4. You are a very rich person who collects non-Western art. Which painting will you buy from the museum?

Reading Reaction

A. Read this selection about a famous, but unusual, artist.

WRAP IT UP

by Vroma Coley

Christo is a famous artist. He was born in Bulgaria in 1935. He specializes in an unusual kind of art. It's not the classical kind of art such as the sculpture *Venus de Milo* or the painting *Mona Lisa,* both of which are centuries old. Christo's art lasts only for a short time—usually only for a few days. What kind of artist is he? Well, he's a wrapper. No, not a *rapper;* that's a musical performer. Christo wraps things. Big things like buildings and monuments. Yes, that's right— buildings and monuments. His wrappings include the Brandenburg Gate in Berlin and the Louvre in Paris. People in the art world still talk about his wrapped islands near Miami. He covered them in flamingo pink plastic.

Before Christo wraps something, he has to study it carefully. He decides on the amount and kind of materials he will use. He also needs a lot of people to help. Many of them are volunteers. Often he has to use large machinery and other equipment. Then, he decides on a price. He finds people who are willing to pay for his work and materials, usually hundreds of thousands of dollars. So, if you want to look at Christo's art, don't look inside a museum. Look outside.

By the way, my sister wraps gifts at K-Mart during the holiday season. Maybe Christo has a job for her. At least I can take her wrappings home with me.

B. Circle *T* if the statement is true or *F* if the statement is false.

1. Christo's art costs a lot of money.   T   F

2. Christo's art will last for centuries.   T   F

3. Christo works alone.   T   F

4. You can find Christo's art in museums.   T   F

5. Christo is from Eastern Europe.   T   F

6. Christo uses different materials to wrap things.   T   F

7. The writer's sister has a job with the artist.   T   F

8. Christo wraps gifts at a department store during the holiday season.   T   F

C. Answer these questions about Christo. Discuss your answers.

1. What is unusual about Christo's art?
2. Where is he from?
3. What are some of his wrappings?
4. What does Christo do before he produces his art?
5. Is this art? Why or why not?

Opinion Survey: The Role of Art

A. Complete this survey. Circle *A* if you agree or *D* if you disagree with the statements.

1. Art is important to society.   A   D
2. Art is *not* the government's responsibility.   A   D
3. Artists are strange, unusual people.   A   D
4. Art is just another business.   A   D
5. Good art has to pass the test of time.   A   D
6. Artists do not have enough money.   A   D
7. The art by a dead artist is worth more than the art of a living artist.   A   D
8. Children need to learn art at an early age.   A   D
9. Men are better artists than women.   A   D
10. Some countries have more art than others.   A   D

B. Compare your answers with a partner. Discuss four statements in more detail.

Written Reaction

A. Match the words and phrases with their meanings.

__c__ 1. portrait   a. the historical period (14th to 17th centuries), when artists used classical styles

_____ 2. geometric   b. literature, usually for children, using simple lines, dots, and colors in pictures

_____ 3. abstract   c. picture of a person

_____ 4. comic book   d. belonging to the same time period

_____ 5. contemporary   e. (to) place an object in paper or other material and tie it up tightly

_____ 6. the Renaissance   f. not realistic; not photographic in details

_____ 7. lifelike   g. realistic; resembling a person or object in art

_____ 8. (to) wrap   h. using angles, shapes, lines, surfaces, and solids in art

B. Write a one-sentence description about each of the paintings on page 8.

Example

Painting A is the most interesting because it is the most abstract.

1. _____

2. _____

3. _____

4. _____

5. _____

6. _____

C. Choose your favorite painting from page 8 and write a paragraph about it. Include a complete description for someone who cannot see it.

D. Write a paragraph to answer the question: "What is art?"

Unit Three

Love Is Blind

Reaction

What feelings do these two people have for each other?
What differences between them do you observe?

Interaction

A. Read the selection "Opposites Attract." How are the people different?

Opposites Attract

Corinne is an unusually tall thirty-four-year-old doctor from a conservative small town. Shy as a young girl, she was the only child of very religious, middle-class parents. As a result, she has a strong sense of morality. Corinne wants to help other people; that's why she decided to study medicine. She worked very hard to become a doctor. She overcame academic problems as well as social difficulties. She is very dedicated to her job, has a reserved personality, and she rarely enjoys herself.

Six months ago, she met a nurse, Fernando, who works in the same area of the hospital. He left the Philippines several years ago. At first, she noticed how short he was, particularly when she stood next to him. Now, after getting to know him, she sees him in a different way: as an outgoing and joyful man. His good sense of humor makes her happy, and she enjoys his company.

Corinne's parents realize that Fernando has a good influence on her, but, for various reasons, they do not approve of him. Corinne told them a lot about him. They know that he comes from a poor family. They also know that he is eight years younger than Corinne. They do not know that he has a two-year-old child from an earlier marriage.

Fernando does not seem to notice all these differences. He wants to marry Corinne, but she is confused. On the one hand, she loves Fernando. On the other hand, she does not want to disappoint her parents.

B. Circle *T* if the statement is true or *F* if the statement is false. If you do not know, circle *?*.

1. Corinne is younger than Fernando.   T   F   ?

2. Fernando is taller than Corinne.   T   F   ?

3. Fernando's parents object to their relationship. T   F   ?

4. Corinne and Fernando have a child.   T   F   ?

5. Corinne wants to marry Fernando.   T   F   ?

6. Both Corinne and Fernando are very religious.   T   F   ?

7. Fernando is more educated than Corinne.   T   F   ?

8. Both work in the medical profession.   T   F   ?

C. Discuss these questions.

1. Why can't Corinne marry Fernando at the present time?
2. Why does Fernando want to marry Corinne?
3. Why does Corinne want to marry Fernando?
4. Why is it important for Corinne to be cautious?
5. Why don't Corinne's parents want her to marry Fernando?
6. How do you think Fernando's family feels about the relationship?
7. In which ways are Corinne and Fernando different?
8. How are Corinne and Fernando similar?

D. In a group, discuss Corinne's options. Agree on one option.

1. Corinne can continue seeing Fernando with no commitments.
2. Corinne can agree to move in with Fernando.
3. Corinne can ask Fernando to move in with her.
4. Corinne can listen to her parents, forget Fernando, and find another person.
5. Corinne can marry Fernando and hope that her parents understand.

E. Answer these questions. Discuss your answers with a partner.

1. When choosing someone for marriage or a long-lasting relationship, is it best to look for a partner with a similar background or a different background?
2. Should the person have similar or different interests?
3. How are marriage customs different throughout the world?
4. What is an arranged marriage?
5. What are some reasons for people to get married?

Pronunciation *a, of,* **and** *to*

In rapid speech, *a* and *of* often sound like *uh; to* sometimes sounds like *tuh.*

1 Listen to your teacher read this dialogue.

FATHER: I don't approve of Fernando.

CORINNE: I know. He's a little younger than I am, but he's such a nice person.

FATHER: O.K. But you're a doctor.

CORINNE: Well, he wants to help people, too. As a matter of fact, he went to night school to become a nurse. That's a good thing, isn't it?

FATHER: What do you want me to say?

2 Repeat the dialogue after your teacher.

3 With a partner, practice the dialogue between Corinne and her father.

Opinion Survey: Marriage

A. Complete this survey. Circle *A* if you agree or *D* if you disagree with the statements.

	A	D
1. It's important for people to marry someone of their own religion.	A	D
2. It's better if people marry someone of the same race.	A	D
3. People should marry within their own social class.	A	D
4. It's O.K. if people with mental disabilities get married.	A	D
5. It's important for two people to love each other before they get married.	A	D
6. It's O.K. if the husband is younger than the wife.	A	D
7. It's O.K. if the wife is more educated than the husband.	A	D
8. It's important for two people to stay in a marriage until death.	A	D
9. It's O.K. for people under eighteen years of age to get married.	A	D
10. Parents should choose a marriage partner for their son or daughter.	A	D

B. Compare your answers with the other students in your class. Find out how many agree or disagree with the statements. Use percentages to report the class's findings.

Example
Eighty percent of the students feel that it's important to marry within their own social class.

Reading Reaction

A. Before you read "Marriage Customs," think about these questions.
- What are some marriage customs that you know of?
- How are marriage customs changing?

Marriage Customs

"Love and marriage go together like a horse and carriage" are the words of a song from an old movie. Throughout the world there are different marriage customs. In Western countries, a man and a woman usually marry after a period of dating. The time they spend together allows them to know each other and to find out if they love each other. Often a wedding is an expensive but happy occasion for the families of the bride and groom. The costs include the decorations and clergy for the ceremony, the gowns and the suits, the music arrangements, the flowers, the photographer, the reception after the marriage ceremony, and the other parties for

(continued)

the bride and groom. Also, many couples rent a limousine for transportation, sometimes even a Mercedes, Lincoln, or Cadillac.

However, it is not necessary to spend so much on a wedding. For those who want to get married quickly and cheaply, there are convenient wedding chapels like those in Las Vegas for "walk-in" weddings. A couple just walks down the aisle where a justice of the peace and a witness are waiting. Even the wedding music is playing. Some of these chapels will show the wedding on the Internet for a small additional charge.

In the Middle East, a man and a woman can get married without even seeing each other. It is a family arrangement. The mother of the unmarried man, through her contacts with other women, looks for a wife for her son. Other mothers recommend their daughters or other young women as possible wives. If the parents agree, they plan the wedding. After the wedding, the couple lives together as husband and wife. Usually the bride has a dowry, a gift for the husband, which often includes money, a place to live, jewelry, or household items. In some tribes in the Sahara Desert, the dowry sometimes includes animals like sheep, goats, or camels. Arranged marriages like these seem to last.

In Japan and other East Asian countries, it is not unusual to have two wedding ceremonies: a Western style ceremony with a white bridal gown, wedding attendants, and a wedding party; and a second Confucian or Buddhist ceremony in traditional dress. Photographers take pictures of both ceremonies and print them in newspapers or display them in their shop windows.

Wherever the location and whatever the custom, marriage is a serious occasion in a couple's life together, and weddings are here to stay. A wedding represents a commitment between two people to share their lives together.

Unfortunately, not all marriages are happy. Not even royal marriages. Everyone remembers the screaming headlines when Prince Charles and Princess Diana divorced. Today more than half the marriages in the United States end in divorce. A divorce court is not a place for love and sharing. A divorce is about money, for the most part. Frequently there are angry arguments between the husband and wife or their lawyers about who gets what or who gets whom when children are involved. At a time like this, one remembers the words of another song, from the musical, *Oliver:* "Where is love? Has it gone so far away?"

B. Circle the words that best complete the sentences or answer the questions.

1. The (husband / mother / wife) usually arranges the marriage in the Middle East.

2. In the Middle East, the wife usually has a (service / dowry / limousine) for the husband.

3. A walk-in wedding does *not* include the (clergy / justice of the peace / music).

4. A Western wedding does *not* usually include (flowers / a reception / a dowry).

5. Which is true? (American marriages have a low rate of divorce. / American weddings are always expensive. / Middle Eastern marriages have a low rate of divorce.)

6. A (divorce / wedding / marriage) is a matter of who gets what.

7. Which is probably *not* a part of a dowry? (A house / A limousine / Jewelry / A camel).

8. Dating before getting married is a (Middle Eastern / Western / Buddhist) custom.

C. Explain the following in your own words.

1. An arranged marriage   3. An East Asian wedding

2. A walk-in wedding   4. A Western wedding

D. Every culture has its own wedding traditions. In a group, tell your classmates about a typical wedding in your country. Include the following information:

1. The preparation and arrangements   7. The party

2. The ceremony   8. The music

3. The guests   9. The decorations (flowers, etc.)

4. The food   10. The clothing

5. The gifts   11. The transportation

6. Superstitions   12. The roles of the members of the wedding

Written Reaction

A. What do you think these words or phrases mean? Discuss your answers.

1. *to grow up*   Is it to become younger or older?

2. *a sense of morality*   Is it having principles or having money?

3. *conservative*   Is it traditional or modern?

4. *to notice*   Is it to perceive or to write something?

5. *although*   Does this mean a similar or a different idea?

6. *to approve*   Does this mean to accept or to refuse?

7. *confused*   Is it a positive or a negative feeling?

8. *to disappoint*   Does this mean to please or not to please?

B. Write five sentences that describe how Corinne and Fernando are different. Use *but, on the other hand,* and *however.*

Example

Corinne is a doctor, but Fernando is a nurse.

1. _____
2. _____
3. _____
4. _____
5. _____

C. Write a paragraph on weddings or marriage customs in your country.

D. Describe your views on marriage. Include some of these topics: age, divorce, social class, education, physical appearance, race, religion, nationality, and language.

Section 2 Fantasy

Unit Four

Desert Dilemma

Reaction

What do you need to survive in a place like this?

What are some dangerous sports people like to do?

Interaction

A. Read about the situation.

You are driving alone through the desert on vacation and your sport utility vehicle (SUV) breaks down late in the afternoon. You cannot fix it. You discover that the road you are traveling on is closed to traffic. What's worse, the road is not even on the map. There is little hope of anyone driving by to help you.

You remember passing a service station. Your best solution is to walk back to the station. You calculate that you have driven about two and a half hours at an average speed of 40 kilometers (25 miles) per hour. You will have to travel only at night because of the intense heat and the burning sun.

B. You have the following items in your SUV.

- a roll of toilet paper
- a mess kit
- a dozen eggs
- a box of powdered milk
- a canteen of water
- a sleeping bag
- a book of matches
- a dozen flares
- a portable radio

- a wool blanket
- a road map
- a first-aid kit
- a large utility knife
- a can of insect repellent
- a one-person tent
- a flare gun
- a flashlight
- a thermos of hot coffee

- a folding camping stove
- a compass
- a kilo (2.2 pounds) of fresh fruit and vegetables
- a beach umbrella
- a cell phone
- three cans of food
- a can opener
- a tube of sun screen lotion

With a partner, put each item into the correct category: *Equipment* or *Food*.

Example

Equipment   *Food*
toilet paper   eggs

C. You can only take five items because of the limitations of space and weight. Make a list of the items to take with you, in order of importance. In a group come to an agreement. Discuss your choices with the class.

D. Discuss these questions with a partner.

1. What are some other items you might need?
2. What alternatives are there for solving this situation other than walking back to the service station?

Reading Reaction

A. Read the selection.

Dangerous Sports

by Oona Fritz

Why do people take risks? Why do they play dangerous sports? When things go wrong, who pays for the rescue? Driving alone through the desert certainly has its dangers. Yet, there are other more dangerous activities—at least five categories of them, depending on where they occur: (1) under the ground, (2) on the ground, (3) under the sea, (4) in the air, or (5) in a combination of these locations.

Spelunking is a sport where explorers go deep inside underground caves that are dark and wet. For an above ground sport there is mountain or rock climbing. These are risky because many climbers, although they are usually careful, fall or are covered in avalanches in bad weather. Many people enjoy scuba diving, which requires special training in the use of oxygen underwater. Surfers get a thrill from the big ocean waves they ride. Bungee jumping is a different kind of thrill. A person tied to an elastic cord jumps from a high place. The cord is just long enough so that it stops the jumper a few inches above the ground below. Hang gliding and sky diving are also unsafe for a thrill seeker since, because of unpredictable air currents, the person cannot always control exactly where the glider or the parachute will come down.

Another dangerous sport in the news recently is hot air ballooning. In April 1999, an Englishman and a Swiss were the first to go around the earth in a hot air balloon. Many other adventurers have tried to do this circumnavigation before. However, they had to be rescued in the Pacific Ocean or in other remote parts of the world.

Perhaps there is a thrill that people get from dangerous sports. Maybe they want more excitement in their lives. Who knows? Nevertheless, these rescues cost thousands of dollars. In addition to ships, planes, and helicopters, other people—expert rescuers— are also involved. They find themselves in the dangerous position of bringing these adventurers back to safety. Even expert mountain climbers on occasion need rescuing, as was the case some years ago on Mt. Everest. So the next time you hear of an adventurer in some dangerous situation, ask yourself: Who's paying for that thrill?

B. Work with a partner. Match the sport with its description. Some sports may be used more than one time.

a. spelunking

b. scuba diving

c. surfing

d. hang gliding

e. sky diving

f. hot air ballooning

g. mountain climbing

h. bungee jumping

_____ 1. an underwater sport
_____ 2. the exploration of caves
_____ 3. an underground sport
_____ 4. an above-the-ground sport
_____ 5. a sport people do in the air
_____ 6. a sport where air currents are a problem
_____ 7. a sport people do on the surface of the water
_____ 8. a sport people do in high places

C. Answer these questions. Discuss your answers.

1. Why do people like dangerous sports?
2. What is bungee jumping?
3. What are some of the dangers of hang gliding and skydiving?
4. What are some other dangerous sports?
5. What equipment is needed for each sport?
6. Which sport do you want to try?
7. Which sport do you not want to try?
8. What does the author mean by *thrill?*

Opinion Survey: Dangerous Sports

A. Complete the survey. Circle *A* if you agree or *D* if you disagree with the statements.

1. People who play dangerous sports should pay for their rescues.	**A**	**D**
2. People with children should not go bungee jumping.	**A**	**D**
3. Bullfighting should be abolished.	**A**	**D**
4. Boxing is too violent.	**A**	**D**
5. Bird-watching is for old people.	**A**	**D**
6. Hunting should be illegal.	**A**	**D**
7. Surfing is only for young people.	**A**	**D**
8. The best way to keep healthy is playing any sport.	**A**	**D**
9. People who play dangerous sports are a little crazy.	**A**	**D**
10. It's O.K. for women and men to play the same sports.	**A**	**D**

B. Compare your answers with a partner. Use verbs such as *think* and *believe* to report your partner's answers to the class.

Example

Guillermo thinks that bullfighting is a traditional sport and should not be abolished.

Pronunciation **Syllables and Stress**

Syllables are a way to divide words into smaller parts. All nouns have syllables that are stressed. Stressed syllables sound louder than the others.

1 Listen to your teacher read these phrases. Write the number of syllables you hear.

a. toilet paper   <u> 4 </u>   f. fresh vegetables   <u>   </u>

b. canned food   <u>   </u>   g. canteen of water   <u>   </u>

c. utility knife   <u>   </u>   h. book of matches   <u>   </u>

d. sunscreen lotion   <u>   </u>   i. a dozen eggs   <u>   </u>

e. flare gun   <u>   </u>   j. powdered milk   <u>   </u>

2 Listen again and underline the stressed syllables in each word.

3 Repeat the phrases after your teacher.

4 With a partner, practice saying the phrases.

Written Reaction

A. Match the words and phrases with their meanings.

_e_ 1. to go wrong   a. far away, not near

_____ 2. categories   b. strong feeling of excitement

_____ 3. unpredictable   c. sorts, kinds

_____ 4. thrill   d. professional

_____ 5. cord   e. not to happen in the desired way

_____ 6. to rescue   f. string or rope

_____ 7. remote   g. cannot be planned on

_____ 8. expert   h. to save someone or something from a dangerous situation.

B. Write sentences about the five items you chose in part C on page 22. Give reasons for each one.

Example

The most important item to take is a compass because you need to know where to walk.

C. Imagine that you are in the desert now. Write a journal entry about what is happening. Write about your choices and your plan of action.

D. Write a newspaper article about a dangerous sport. Create your own title.

The Murder of the Earl of Hereford

Reaction

Which room is this?
A murder is about to happen. Guess how the person will die.

Interaction

A. Read about the situation.

Someone calls the police to the house of the strange and rich Earl of Hereford. He is dead. The police suspect that someone poisoned him during dinner by putting something into his wine. There are three guests at the table. They refuse to talk to the police. So the police must solve this crime themselves, but they have a lot of information (clues).

CLUES

1. The maid was not working that evening.
2. All three guests are members of the earl's strange family.
   One is a mad scientist.
   One is a professional weight lifter.
   One is a fashion model.
3. One of the guests has only a right arm.
4. The model does not eat meat.
5. The professional weight lifter sat opposite the earl.
6. The mad scientist is married to a vegetarian.
7. The earl's nephew does not drink alcohol.
8. The mad scientist sat to the right of the earl.
9. The weight lifter is a teetotaler.
10. The earl is left handed.
11. The model has a beard.
12. The cat was asleep in the late afternoon sunlight behind the earl's chair.
13. The married couple are the earl's daughter and son-in-law.
14. The vegetarian is right handed.

B. Discuss these questions with a partner.

1. Where was each person sitting? Write their names on the drawing.
2. Where was the cat? Draw the cat on the floor plan. Why is the location of the cat important?
3. How many men and women were at the table? Describe each one with all the details you know.
4. How is each person related to the earl?
5. Who probably killed the earl? Why do you think that person killed him?
6. What seems strange, unusual, or surprising to you about the earl's family?

Reading Reaction

A. Before you read the following selection, think about these questions.

- Who is probably the greatest leader in the last thousand years?
- Can a woman lead as well as a man?

What She Did for Love

by Roy L. Sporter

Elizabeth I was queen of England from 1558 to 1603. She became queen after the death of her father, Henry VIII. Although her childhood was difficult (her mother was killed and she spent a lot of time alone), she became a very strong queen. She gave up much for her people. In fact, she felt like one of them, moving easily among them. She never married and never had children. She probably never even had a lover. She was named "the virgin queen," and this description of her was how the colonial state of Virginia got its name.

She was married to England. While she was queen, the country changed from a small, insignificant country to a world power. English culture and language spread to various parts of the world, and the arts flourished. Shakespeare wrote his dramatic masterpieces while she was queen. Her powerful navy ruled the seas and defeated the Spanish navy, then the strongest in the world, in 1588. Her handmade dresses were complex works of art, and she took great care with her appearance. Other world leaders of her time, even her enemies, respected her as a wise and excellent ruler. What's more, she ruled England at a time when women played no part in political affairs. Recently *The New York Times Magazine* called her "the best leader" of the millennium.

Toward the end of her forty-five-year reign, the old and feeble queen spoke one last time to Parliament. Her words were something like this: "You have had and will have many wiser and stronger rulers sitting in this seat." she continued, "but you have never had nor will you ever have anyone who will love you better."

Although there were scandals during Elizabeth's reign, her time seems mild compared to the royal happenings today. What was her secret? Why was she such an effective queen? Maybe her secret was simple: She truly loved and trusted her people. Does that ring a bell? Wasn't Princess Diana called "the people's princess" after her divorce from Prince Charles?

B. Circle *T* if the statement is true or *F* if the statement is false. If you do not know, circle *?*.

1. Elizabeth I was like kings and queens of today.   T   F   ?
2. The people loved Elizabeth I.   T   F   ?
3. Elizabeth I visited many parts of the world.   T   F   ?
4. Her friends and enemies respected her.   T   F   ?
5. She increased English influence throughout the world.   T   F   ?
6. She was close to her mother.   T   F   ?
7. She was a very religious person.   T   F   ?
8. Her father trained her to be queen.   T   F   ?

C. Answer these questions. Discuss your answers with a partner.

1. When was Elizabeth I queen of England?
2. What did she give up in order to be queen?
3. How did she feel about her subjects?
4. What are some of her accomplishments?
5. What happened during her reign?
6. What was her probable secret in being a good ruler?
7. Who is Elizabeth I compared to in the reading?

Opinion Survey: The Upper Class

A. Complete this survey. Circle *A* if you agree or *D* if you disagree with the statements.

1. Kings and queens have little usefulness today.   A   D
2. Having royal blood is better than being rich.   A   D
3. The amount of money you have is important in society.   A   D
4. Society has a double standard: one for the rich and another for the poor.   A   D
5. Royal people are usually strange and don't understand the common people.   A   D
6. Money makes you happy.   A   D
7. It's better to work for one's money instead of getting it from your family.   A   D
8. Royal people deserve honor and respect.   A   D
9. It's O.K. if the royal people don't pay taxes.   A   D
10. The monarch does not always have to be the firstborn male.   A   D

B. Compare your answers with the other students in your class. Find out how many agree or disagree with the statements. Use numbers to report your class's opinions.

Example

Nine out of ten students agree with the statement that kings and queens have little usefulness today.

Pronunciation | **Stress in Noun Phrases**

A noun phrase contains a noun and other words. Sometimes these words are adjectives, other nouns, or adverbs. Stressed syllables sound louder than the others.

1 Listen to your teacher read these phrases.

a. a <u>right</u>-<u>hand</u>ed vege<u>tar</u>ian

b. the virgin queen

c. a professional weight lifter

d. a world power

e. a fashion model

f. *The New York Times Magazine*

g. a very strong ruler

h. other world leaders

i. a forty-five-year reign

j. the earl's strange family

2 Listen again and underline the stressed syllables in each phrase.

3 Repeat the phrases after your teacher.

4 With a partner, practice saying the phrases.

Written Reaction

A. Complete this paragraph. Use the words in the box that best match the meanings under each blank.

effective	insignificant	reign	monarch
flourished	mighty	mild	

When Elizabeth I began her _____, England was a(n)
                  1. time as queen or king

_____ country. She became an effective _____, and the
  2. unimportant   3. royal ruler

Elizabethan years were a golden age: The arts _____ and her
                    4. grew in a healthy state

_____ navy ruled the seas. She gave herself unselfishly to her people. Her
5. having a lot of strength

reign seems _____ by today's standards. No doubt Elizabeth was a(n)
      6. gentle, peaceful

_____ queen, who loved her people.
   7. competent, capable

B. Write five sentences about the earl's family. Use the expression *It is* with the following words: *strange, weird, unusual, unexpected,* and *surprising.*

Example

It is surprising that the earl's daughter is a mad scientist.

1. _____
2. _____
3. _____
4. _____
5. _____

C. Write a police report of the murder. Mention (1) who probably murdered the earl, (2) the way the murder was done, (3) the reason for the murder, (4) the other people involved, (5) their descriptions, and (6) the reasons they are not suspects. Create your own title.

D. Write your opinion of royalty. Answer the question: "Should people from royal families receive special treatment?"

Unit Six

The Jewels Are Missing!

Reaction

Who probably lives in a place like the one in the picture?
What kind of crime is about to happen?

Interaction

A. Read about the situation.

In the sitting room of Dame Dora's eighteenth-century house, the butler, Mr. Ives, is serving drinks. Five people are in the room, including the butler. Someone is about to take the family jewels from the wall safe, which everyone knows how to open. What else is going on?

1. Baroness Lamunda is whispering in the Baron Lamunda's ear.
2. The person in military boots is sipping a glass of sherry.
3. Dame Dora's niece is sitting opposite her aunt.
4. The tea drinker takes the cream and sugar from the man having coffee.
5. The cat is in the lap of Colonel Headstrong, who is petting it.
6. Ives enters with a glass of lemonade for the person to the right of Baroness Lamunda.
7. Suddenly the lights go out, and the guests are startled.
8. The coffee drinker, who writes mysteries, swoons into the arms of the tea drinker.
9. Dame Dora faints.
10. No one hears any footsteps.
11. When Ives finally turns the lights back on, the jewels are gone.

B. Circle *T* if the statement is true or *F* if the statement is false. If you do not know, circle ?.

1. The colonel is a sherry drinker.	T F ?
2. The baroness is a tea drinker.	T F ?
3. All the guests are unable to move.	T F ?
4. Dame Dora's niece is wearing military boots.	T F ?
5. Dame Dora is petting the cat.	T F ?
6. All the people in the room are sitting down.	T F ?

C. Discuss these questions with a partner.

1. How many people are there in this mystery? Name them.
2. What is each person drinking?
3. Where is each person sitting? Write their names on the drawing.
4. What is the niece's occupation? Is this surprising to you?
5. Who faints? Is this surprising to you?
6. Who turned out the lights?
7. Who probably took the jewels?
8. What are some reasons for this robbery?
9. What social class do these people belong to? How do you know? List some reasons.
10. How could Dame Dora have prevented the robbery?

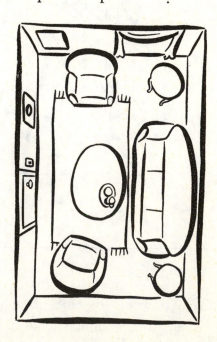

D. Role Play: Work with a partner. One of you is the police investigator and the other is one of the people at Dame Dora's house during the robbery. The police investigator must ask the person questions about the following points.

1. Each person's identity
2. Where each person is sitting
3. What each person is drinking
4. What each person was doing
5. The sequence of events
6. The identification of the thief
7. The reason for your identification

E. Circle how you feel about each of the items in the list. 1 = very valuable; 2 = valuable; 3 = not very valuable.

1 2 3 insurance policies	1 2 3 last will and testament
1 2 3 wedding pictures	1 2 3 gun
1 2 3 deeds to the house and land	1 2 3 title to the car
1 2 3 family recipes	1 2 3 passport/birth certificate
1 2 3 high school/college diploma	1 2 3 tax records
1 2 3 baby's first pair of shoes	1 2 3 photo of baby's first haircut
1 2 3 Mom's jewelry	1 2 3 Grandpa's pocket watch
1 2 3 citizenship/social security papers	1 2 3 photo of an important event in your child's life

F. Write down three other items you value.

1. _____

2. _____

3. _____

G. Decide on five items to put in a wall safe in your home. Compare your list with a partner's list. Discuss the reasons for your choices.

Reading Reaction

A. Before reading, think about these questions.

- What are your favorite memories of your grandmother or grandfather?
- Where did they keep important family papers and other valuable items?

Grandma's Safe

I used to visit my grandmother a few times a year. That was the best I could do because I lived so far away. When she was in her early eighties, still living alone on the family farm, which she called "the old home place," she often reminded me of her "important papers." She did not have a wall safe to keep her papers and valuables in. But she had a refrigerator. Taking my hand, she guided me over to that big white appliance in the corner of her kitchen, opened the door, and dug into the freezer section. There behind some frozen vegetables and meats, she reached for a metal box. It was not a safe.

Actually, it was a Zesta cracker box from the days when crackers came in metal containers. She pulled open the top, but she never actually showed me the contents. She told me what was inside: the birth certificates of all her children, her wedding certificate, the deeds to the farm, her last will and testament, and her living will (she did not want the doctors to continue her life by extraordinary means if she got very sick). I never questioned her further about the contents of the Zesta cracker box.

When she died at 88, the family asked my older brother, who also knew of the Zesta cracker box, to go through the contents. He gently opened the box and unwrapped the plastic bag held tight with a thick rubber band, just as Grandma left it. He slowly poured out the contents on the kitchen table. We all sat around in anticipation. Sure enough, all her legal papers were there; her last will and testament stated that after her death, she wanted everything divided equally among her children. There were also some other items that caught our attention. Inside was some of her jewelry, her gold wedding ring with its modest single diamond and her dainty Elgin watch that Grandpa had given her. We thought they were lost. There were also the old, yellowed photos of her parents and her children, newspaper announcements of family deaths and marriages, and countless other items crammed into that Zesta cracker box. That box was my grandmother's biography. Each item marked a different time in her life.

One item touched us all. Inside a package of taped envelopes, she had placed seeds from her garden. Two envelopes contained snapdragon and larkspur seeds from her grandmother. Another was labeled: "cucumber seeds for the family recipe for bread-and-butter pickles." We divided up the seeds among the family. My flower seeds are blooming in the garden now. As Grandma probably wanted, I will save seeds from my garden for my children. Thank you, Grandma, for your Zesta cracker box. Just as those seeds live, you also live—in us.

B. **Match the words or phrases from the reading with their descriptions.**

  _d_   1. "the old home place"

       2. Zesta cracker box

       3. newspaper announcements

       4. last will and testament

       5. living will

       6. refrigerator

       7. deed

       8. taped-sealed envelopes

a. located in the corner of Grandma's kitchen

b. told of weddings and deaths in the family

c. contained Grandma's request that she did not want unusual efforts to continue her life if she was very sick

d. the farm where Grandma lived

e. metal container that was Grandma's safe

f. legal paper showing Grandma's ownership of the farm

g. contained flower and vegetable seeds from the family farm

h. legal paper that stated that all Grandma's possessions would be divided equally among her heirs.

C. **Answer these questions. Discuss your answers with a partner.**

1. Where did Grandma keep her important papers?
2. Where did she keep the metal box?
3. What kind of metal box was it?
4. What other items did Grandma have in the box?
5. What were Grandma's wishes in her last will and testament? In her living will?
6. What surprise was in the box?
7. What did the writer do with that surprise?
8. How did the writer feel about Grandma's surprise?

Opinion Survey: What Do You Value?

A. **Complete the survey. Circle A if you agree or D if you disagree with the statements.**

It is important for me to:

1. show respect for older people.	A	D
2. wear expensive clothing and jewelry.	A	D
3. go out with attractive people.	A	D
4. be like my friends.	A	D
5. do well in school or in my job.	A	D
6. drive a nice car.	A	D
7. be honest.	A	D
8. listen to my parents.	A	D
9. obey the law.	A	D
10. practice religion.	A	D

B. Compare your answers with a partner's. Report your answers and your partner's answers to the class using expressions such as *both . . . and, neither . . . nor,* and *but.*

Examples

Neither Amelia nor I think that it's important to wear expensive clothes.

Enrique thinks it is important to practice religion, but I don't.

Pronunciation   **Even More on Stress**

All nouns, including nouns used as adjectives, have syllables that are stressed.

❶ Listen to your teacher read the questions and answers. Underline the stressed syllables.

 a. <u>Who</u> <u>drinks</u> <u>coffee</u>?   A <u>coffee</u> <u>drinker</u>
 b. Who loves cars?   A car lover
 c. Who investigates crimes?   A crime investigator
 d. Who drives a truck?   A truck driver
 e. Who plays tennis?   A tennis player

❷ Repeat the questions and answers after your teacher.

❸ With a partner, practice the questions and answers.

Written Reaction

A. Match the words and phrases with their meanings.

  __h__ 1. lap
  _____ 2. startled
  _____ 3. (to) investigate
  _____ 4. last will and testament
  _____ 5. insurance policies
  _____ 6. title to the car
  _____ 7. deed to the house
  _____ 8. tax records

 a. (to) look at the facts; (to) search for the cause of a crime
 b. official papers for paying money to or receiving it from the government
 c. official papers to show ownership for the place where you live
 d. official papers to show ownership of your automobile
 e. official papers to show money paid for health or life benefits
 f. official paper to show what to do with someone's property after death
 g. surprised
 h. a person's upper legs and lower stomach where a child or animal can sit

B. Write five sentences describing what is going on in Dame Dora's house.

Example

While the butler is serving drinks, Colonel Headstrong is petting the cat.

1. _____

2. _____

3. _____

4. _____

5. _____

C. Imagine that you are the crime investigator. Write a crime report about these topics:

- the different people in the room
- their drinks
- their activities
- the seating arrangement
- the thief

D. Write a paragraph about a memory you have of one of your grandparents.

Unit Seven

Slow Business

Reaction

What do you see in this picture?

Where might you find these things?

Interaction

A. Read about the situation.

You are the supervisor at the Shur-Time Watch Company. You have to fire at least one worker because business is slow. The fired worker will receive two weeks' notice and two weeks' extra pay.

	OTTO	NILDA	VERA	PHIL
Education	high-school dropout	high-school graduate	high-school equivalency	high-school graduate; some college
Age	27	21	34	23
Marital Status	single; supports his mother	engaged	single mother with two small children	single; lives with male roommate
Appearance	neat and clean	attractive; well dressed	overweight with long, red fingernails	dresses in bright colors
Personality	pleasant; sometimes late; helpful	outgoing and enthusiastic; talkative	seems tired and bored, uncooperative	happy-go-lucky man
Work Record	slow but good worker; accepted by co-worker;	average worker; frequently late; liked by others	uninterested in her job; often late; absent a lot; argues with others	good worker; helps others; always on time; cooperative
Background	disabled; walks with a cane	little experience; limited English skills	was on public assistance; little prior work experience	good work history; was in a fight once
Future	would like to get a better job with the company	wants to marry and have children	works only because of new government law; prefers to be at home with her children	wants to stay with the company and design watches
Other Comments	because of disability, government helps to pay some of his salary	her uncle is a company director	Shur-Time hired her because of government law to get people off public assistance	although a valued worker, does Shur-Time want to keep someone who fights?

After you read the information in the chart, discuss these questions with a partner.

1. What are the strengths and weaknesses of each worker?
2. Which worker would you fire? Why?
3. In case the company's business gets even worse and you have to fire several workers, rank all the workers. Which one will you fire first? Second? Third? Fourth?
4. Firing a worker is usually difficult because of the worker's personal circumstances. What will happen to Shur-Time's workers if they lose their jobs?

Reading Reaction

A. Before you read the following article, think about these questions.

- What are you wearing that is *not* made in this country?
- Who probably made it? Where? Under what circumstances?

WORKERS OF THE WORLD

Workers in developing countries are not highly paid. For that reason, more and more international companies are setting up factories in areas of the world where workers will work for low pay.

For example, a well-known company that makes very expensive athletic shoes (around $150 a pair) pays its workers in the Far East less than $5.00 a day. When people in the United States learned of the workers' situation, there was an angry reaction. Some sympathetic consumers refused to buy the shoes. A millionaire basketball player, who appears in the company's TV advertisements, stated, "I'm not involved in labor decisions. I just sell sneakers, and the company pays me well." Someone from the company, in response to the scandal, said, "Well, if our company weren't there, the people wouldn't have any jobs. We're making jobs for people who need them."

Perhaps. But what kind of jobs? Low-paying jobs, usually in crowded factories that have little air and poor lighting. The workers do not have benefits like health insurance and life insurance. There is no job security, so that workers are afraid of being fired for any reason at any time. Furthermore, in most cases workers are paid, not an hourly wage, but according to the number of items they produce. As a result, the workers are under great pressure to produce more and more.

Another situation recently in the news involved a television personality who owned part of a children's clothing company. A scandal arose when people learned that the factory in Central America employed children. When the TV personality found out about this, she started an organization that asks people not to buy products made by children.

The next time you buy designer clothing, electronic products, an oriental rug, or any other products manufactured in a developing country, ask yourself: "Who made this?" "What were their working conditions?" "How much money does the company pay the worker?" If you are not happy with the answers, don't buy the product! Write a letter to the company and express your feelings.

B. Circle *T* if the statement is true or *F* if the statement is false. If you do not know, circle *?*.

1. Companies are setting up factories in order to help foreign workers. T F ?

2. Workers in sneaker factories in the Far East are not paid enough. T F ?

3. The person from the company believes that any job is better than no job at all. T F ?

4. Most factories in developing countries are new. T F ?

5. Many foreign factory workers do not have job security. T F ?

6. Foreign factory workers usually receive an hourly wage. T F ?

7. Children work in factories in some developing countries. T F ?

8. The author suggests not buying products from companies that abuse workers. T F ?

C. Answer these questions. Discuss your answers with a partner.

1. Where are workers exploited?

2. In which ways are workers exploited?

3. What sort of product do they make?

4. What do some companies say about their practices?

5. What can consumers do about worker exploitation?

Pronunciation *Will*

In rapid speech, *will* often sounds like the *ul* in *pull*.

1 Listen to your teacher read this dialogue.

MAGGIE: What'll happen to me? I don't have a job.

JUAN: Don't worry. You'll get another one.

MAGGIE: I hope so. How'll I pay my rent? I won't go on welfare.

JUAN: I'll ask my boss if she needs anyone.

MAGGIE: Oh, thanks. That'll help.

2 Repeat the dialogue after your teacher.

3 With a partner, practice the dialogue between Maggie and Juan.

Opinion Survey: A Day's Work

A. Complete the survey. Circle *P* if the statements are personal, *J* if they are job related, or *?* if they are not part of a job description but are helpful in your job.

	P	J	?
1. Keep the work area neat.	P	J	?
2. Remember the boss's birthday.	P	J	?
3. Take telephone messages for your coworkers.	P	J	?
4. Work overtime if necessary.	P	J	?
5. Be on time.	P	J	?
6. If you're getting coffee, offer to get some for others.	P	J	?
7. Don't spend too much time in the restroom.	P	J	?
8. Dress neatly and appropriately at all times.	P	J	?
9. Put things back where they belong.	P	J	?
10. Report to the boss if any other worker does something wrong.	P	J	?

B. In a group, compare your answers with your classmates' answers. Find out how many think the statements are personal, job related, or helpful to your job. Report the results to the rest of the class. Look at these examples.

Examples

I think it's important for my job to keep the work area neat, and most other students agree.

Most of the students think remembering your boss's birthday is personal.

Written Reaction

A. Match the words and phrases with their meanings.

   b   1. (to) underpay   a. (to) start, build

           2. (to) set up   b. (to) pay a low salary

           3. benefits   c. not present; not on the job

           4. absent   d. work (n.)

           5. consumers   e. users, buyers of products

           6. labor   f. unfair treatment

           7. job security   g. life/health insurance, etc., given by an employer to a worker

           8. injustice   h. certainty that one cannot be fired without a good reason

B. Write sentences stating the major strength of each of the workers on page 41.

Example

Otto's major strength is that he's a good worker.

C. Write sentences stating the major weakness of each of the workers on page 41.

Example

Vera's major weakness is that she is uncooperative.

D. Write a letter to the millionaire basketball player mentioned in the reading on page 42 and tell him your opinion about the practices of the athletic shoe company he represents.

Unit Eight

Making a Living

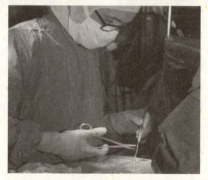

Reaction

Which jobs are exciting?

Which job would you most like to have? Why?

Which job would you least like to have? Why?

Interaction

A. Look at the photos on page 46. Ask and answer questions about what each person does. Use some of the words in exercise B below.

Example

STUDENT A: What does the person in the first picture do?

STUDENT B: He is a zookeeper.

B. Read the list of jobs. Circle *W* if you think the job is good for women, *M* if you think it is good for men, or *E* for either men or women. In a group, compare your answers.

1. Teacher	**W**	**M**	**E**
2. Surgeon	**W**	**M**	**E**
3. Traveling salesperson	**W**	**M**	**E**
4. Zookeeper	**W**	**M**	**E**
5. Mortician	**W**	**M**	**E**
6. Computer technician	**W**	**M**	**E**
7. Professional athlete	**W**	**M**	**E**
8. Airline pilot	**W**	**M**	**E**
9. Social worker/counselor	**W**	**M**	**E**
10. Firefighter	**W**	**M**	**E**
11. Farmer	**W**	**M**	**E**

C. Discuss these questions in a small group.

1. Do you feel that certain jobs are for men? For women? Why?
2. Does the age of the worker make a difference for a job?
3. Which jobs require highly trained workers or workers with special skills?
4. Which jobs require a certain mental stability?
5. Which jobs are best for certain personality types, for example, an outgoing person or a shy person?
6. What educational training is necessary for each job? Which jobs require a lot of experience?
7. Compare the different salaries for these jobs. Which is probably the highest-paying job? The lowest-paying job?
8. Other than money, what rewards do you want from a job?

D. Work in a small group. Imagine that you are managing a new software manufacturing company. Discuss these questions.

1. How many hours per week will the employees work?
2. How much will they receive for overtime work?
3. What will the minimum wage per hour be?
4. Will the company pay for maternity/paternity leave?
5. Will the company pay for health insurance and sick leave?
6. Will the company offer a retirement plan?
7. Will the company hire part-time workers to cut down costs?
8. Will the company start a factory in a foreign country, where wages are lower?
9. How old will the workers be? What are the minimum and maximum ages?
10. How much salary will managers and executives receive?
11. Will the company make special arrangements for disabled workers?
12. Will the company offer stock options to the workers instead of high salaries?

E. Choose a job that you would like to have, and discuss your reasons for choosing this job. Also, discuss the job's importance to society.

Opinion Survey: Job Expectations

A. Complete the survey. Circle *A* if you agree or *D* if you disagree with the statements.

1. The most important factor in a job is the salary.	A	D
2. Women are better at some jobs than men.	A	D
3. Age is not important for a job.	A	D
4. The government should pay extra to help people with physical or mental disabilities work.	A	D
5. A person's salary depends on the amount of education they have completed.	A	D
6. After several years in the same job, a person has job security.	A	D
7. Women need maternity leave with pay.	A	D
8. How well you work is more important than how much you work.	A	D
9. Workers need retirement and health plans with their jobs.	A	D
10. It's O.K. if companies hire part-time workers.	A	D

B. Compare your answers with the other students in your class. Find out how many agree or disagree with the statements. Use fractions to report your class's opinions.

Example

Three-quarters of the class agree that the salary is the most important thing in a job.

Reading Reaction

A. Before you read the selection, think about these questions.

- What are the traditional roles of women? Of men?
- Can men perform roles traditionally held by women?
- Can women perform roles traditionally held by men?

What Is Sexism? An Interview with Sociologist Frieda M. Fall

What is sexism? It involves discrimination and is based on the belief that one sex is inferior. Sexism affects both men and women because either can be the object of discrimination. Nevertheless, most sexism is usually against women.

Where does it exist? Sexism occurs all over the world, but research shows it is more common in developing countries that have few well-educated women.

What are the traditional roles for men and women? Men have traditionally been the breadwinners. Therefore, they tend to be more assertive and ambitious. On the other hand, women have traditionally been homemakers. Their role has been to focus on their families' wants and needs and to be compassionate and supportive. Consequently, members of the two sexes have behaved differently.

Are these roles the same all over the world? No. They are different in some societies, though they are similar in many societies.

How do we learn our gender roles? Through interaction with the family, peers, school, and through the process of becoming aware of ourselves.

(continued)

Do working women have equality with men? No. Women still often work in lower prestige jobs and are paid less than men.

Do women today do as well as men in education? Yes and no. In attending and graduating from college, women do as well or better than men. Yet in many high school subjects, girls get lower scores in many subjects than boys.

What are women's accomplishments in politics? They are better off than before, but they still do not have equality with men. More men are elected to political office.

What about women in religion? Many religions do not accept women as leaders, and they are often seen as inferior to men. Many religious traditions require women to obey their husbands.

Are women biologically inferior to men? No. In some ways women are superior to men and in other ways inferior.

Why should we know about sexism? Because your mother is a woman. Don't let anyone mistreat her!

B. Circle the correct answer. Some questions have more than one correct answer.

1. Sexism is (never/only/sometimes) against men.

2. Sexism is most noticeable in (American/developing/developed) countries.

3. Women are (not supposed to be/supposed to be/usually) supportive in traditional roles.

4. In traditional societies men's and women's roles are (different/similar/the same).

5. Gender roles are usually not learned from (peers/school/tradition/family).

6. Women usually (are treated equally to/get paid less money than/have higher-prestige jobs than) men.

C. Answer these questions. Discuss your answers in a small group.

1. What is sexism?

2. Who are the victims of sexism?

3. Where does sexism most frequently occur?

4. From which sources do we learn our gender roles?

5. Which prejudices exist against women? Against men?

6. How have women done in education, jobs, religion, and politics?

Pronunciation   Do you

In rapid speech, *do you* often sounds like *d'ya.*

1 Listen to your teacher read this dialogue.

MARIKO: Where do you live?

LEE: I live in Pinewood.

MARIKO: Who do you live with?

LEE: My brother. He's a student. Do you live with your family?

MARIKO: No, but I have a roommate.

LEE: What do you do?

MARIKO: I'm a computer technician.

2 Repeat the dialogue after your teacher.

3 With a partner, practice the dialogue.

Written Reaction

A. Fill in the blanks with the correct words from the box.

minimum wage	retirement plan	mentally or physically disabled	mistreat
ambitious	inferior	gender roles	accomplishment

1. Many companies offer a _____ for workers after they stop working with the company.
2. Some good workers may have handicaps like being _____ .
3. The least amount of money that an employer can pay workers legally is called a _____ .
4. When you want to get ahead in your career, you are _____ .
5. Some people believe that women are _____ to men, that is, that women are not as qualified as men.
6. Some companies _____ their workers by paying them low salaries and offering no benefits.
7. We learn _____ , that is, stereotypical roles for men and women, from family, school, and other influences.
8. Today more women serve in political positions, which is a(n) _____ to be proud of.

B. Write a paragraph on the differences or similarities between men and women. Create your own title. Mention the following topics:
- biological differences/similarities between men and women
- roles in society
- differences/similarities in jobs
- accomplishments in politics

Hot Lines!

Reaction

What is happening in this picture?
Who are these people and what do they want?

Interaction

A. Read the newspaper article.

SUSPICIOUS FIRE AT AMBITEL

A suspicious fire destroyed the main office in the Ambivalent Telephone Company (AMBITEL) last night. The local fire department put out the fire just after midnight. According to the police the fire is under investigation because of a labor dispute at AMBITEL. Workers are on strike for higher salaries and better benefits. Police are questioning the only people who were in the AMBITEL building late last night.

A. X. Bellhead   Di Eltone   Bea Z. Lyons   Trunk Lyons   Lon D. Stanz

B. Read the information from the police investigation. There are statements from the five suspects who were in the AMBITEL building last night. The police interviewed the suspects separately. Then, read the time sheet from the company on page 55.

Statements from Suspects

A. X. Bellhead

"I'm the president of AMBITEL. I have to make the difficult decisions. Last night I had a long meeting with Ms. Lyons until just after 10 P.M. I told her that I was planning to hire new workers if this strike didn't stop. The union's demands will cause customers to pay more, and they're not going to like it."

Di Eltone

"I'm A. X.'s—er, Mr. Bellhead's—secretary. I'd do anything for him. I worked late last night—until around 10. Bea and Trunk were in a meeting with Mr. Bellhead. I heard them yelling loudly at each other. I left just before they left."

Bea Z. Lyons

"I'm the head of the AMBITEL workers' union, and I've worked here for twenty-nine years. My son and I met briefly with A. X. last night. It was around half past ten when the meeting ended. If this strike continues much longer, A. X. is going to lose his job. He'll do anything to prevent that. He doesn't care about the workers."

Trunk Lyons

"I'm Trunk Lyons, Mrs. Lyons's son. I'm also her assistant. She's going to retire next year, and she wants me to take over. But some people think I'm not qualified. By the way, I don't know anything about a fire. My mother and I left at the same time—by the back door. It was about 10:30."

Lon D. Stanz

"I was the security guard on duty last night at the entrance. It was a quiet night. The last thing I remember is saying good night to Mr. Bellhead around 10:15. A little later, I heard footsteps. Then someone hit me from behind with a heavy object. When I came to, I smelled a woman's perfume."

NAME	COMPANY	TIME IN	TIME OUT	SIGNATURE
A. X. Bellhead	AMBITEL	8:45 A.m.	10:15 P.m.	*A. X. Bellhead*
Pitt Bradley	Pan-Artists	8:00 P.M.	10:00 P.M.	*Pitt Bradley*
Di Eltone	AMBITEL	8:30 A.m.		
Regina Hall	Graph INC	9:00 A.m.	5:10 P.m.	*Regina Hall*
Bea Z. Lyons	AMBITEL	8:40 A.m.		
Trunk Lyons	AMBITEL	10:15 A.m.		
Hana Viceroy	Pan-Artists	9:15 A.M.	6:10 P.M.	*Hana Viceroy*

C. **Match the following characters with some of their characteristics. Some have more than one answer.**

<u>e, g, h</u> 1. A. X. Bellhead   a. the head of the AMBITEL union

_____ 2. Di Eltone   b. the security guard

_____ 3. Bea Z. Lyons   c. the earliest AMBITEL worker to sign in

_____ 4. Trunk Lyons   d. did not sign out

_____ 5. Lon D. Stanz   e. the head of AMBITEL

                                    f. Mr. Bellhead's secretary

                                    g. the last AMBITEL worker to sign out

                                    h. left by the main entrance

                                    i. place of departure not known

D. **With a partner, discuss the questions about these topics.**

The Fire	• How do you think the fire started? • About what time do you think the fire started?
The Background	• What was the labor dispute about? • Why didn't Mr. Bellhead agree to the workers' demands? • What were the plans of Ms. Lyons's son?
The Time	• What time did the firefighters put out the fire? • What time did the meeting end? • What time did Mr. Bellhead leave? Ms. Lyons? Mr. Lyons? Ms. Eltone?
The People	• Who was in the meeting? • What was each person doing before the fire?
The Differences	• What were the differences between Mr. Bellhead's statement and Ms. Lyons's? • What were the differences between Ms. Eltone's statement and Mr. Stanz's? • What were the differences between Mr. Lyons's statement and Ms. Eltone's?

E. **Who did it? Who started the fire? With a group discuss the reasons for your suspicions.**

Opinion Survey: Workers and Management

A. Complete this survey. Circle *A* if you agree or *D* if you disagree with the statements.

1. Company managers have too much power.	A	D
2. Union leaders are dishonest.	A	D
3. There is no need for unions today.	A	D
4. Company managers need workers to help them run the company.	A	D
5. Strikes cause more harm than good.	A	D
6. Workers in hospitals, schools, and other public areas should *not* go on strike.	A	D
7. It's O.K. to hire nonunion workers.	A	D
8. Unions are only for workers on a salary.	A	D
9. Union dues should be set according to a worker's salary.	A	D
10. Union leaders should fight for more benefits for the employees.	A	D

B. Compare your answers with a partner's. Discuss four statements in more detail.

Reading Reaction

A. Before you read this selection, think about these questions.
- What were working conditions like a long time ago?
- What are some of the memories about work that your older relatives have?

A Working Woman

by Susan B. Anderson

My great-grandmother Sarah was a working woman. She was a union organizer in the South. I remember her many stories about organizing the workers. In those days most workers in the South did not receive good salaries. Most of them worked in cotton or textile mills, making thread or cloth from cotton. After tobacco, cotton was the main crop in the South. For these workers, there were neither health nor retirement benefits. When people got too old to work in the mills, their families had to take care of them. Many workers did not live to retire because of "brown lung," a

(continued)

disease that the workers developed by breathing the cotton fibers in the mills. Gramma Sarah always sent these sick people to the town doctor, but he did very little. He was, after all, also the company doctor.

Since there were no laws to limit the total number of work hours, people often worked 10 to 12 hours per day. There was neither overtime nor vacation. Women workers had a very hard time. Those who had young children rushed home to feed them during their lunchtime. The men were a bit better off: They received better salaries, while women, who often did the same jobs, received less. One horrible story that I heard repeatedly involved a young girl who fell into one of these big machines and died from her injuries. Every time Gramma Sarah told the story, her voice broke and her eyes filled with tears. Then, there was silence as she looked away—into the distant past with its painful memories.

As a union organizer, Gramma Sarah was not very successful. Not one of her mills voted for the union. She said the workers were afraid because the mill owners threatened to close the mills. Those who were sympathetic received warnings or lost their jobs. Anti-union gangs beat them and burned their houses. It was dangerous to be pro-union in those days.

But maybe she *was* successful in a way. Although none of her mills accepted a union, other mills were unionized. As a result, all mill workers benefited. Nonunion mills knew that they had to offer the same benefits as unionized mills in order to keep good workers. As Gramma Sarah said, "Things are different for cotton mill workers now." At least in this country.

B. Draw a line through the *incorrect* answer(s). Some statements may have more than one answer.

1. Gramma Sarah was (anti-union / a working woman / a union organizer).
2. Cotton mill workers did *not* have (health benefits / lunchtimes / good salaries).
3. (Cotton / tobacco / corn) was one of the main crops in the South.
4. When workers got too old to work, (their families cared for them / they often developed brown lung / they retired on a pension).
5. Gramma Sarah was (successful / hardworking / unsympathetic).
6. (Owners threatened to close the mills / Mill workers were afraid / A child fell into a machine) as a result of the union activity.

C. Answer these questions. Discuss your answers.

1. What is "brown lung"?
2. How were the workers mistreated?
3. What sort of life did female mill workers have?
4. What story did Gramma Sarah tell? How did she tell the story?
5. What happened to workers who were in favor of a union?
6. How was Gramma Sarah's life successful?

Pronunciation | **Personal Pronouns**

In rapid speech, personal pronouns after verbs or prepositions are used as objects and are usually unstressed: *her* often sounds like *er, him* like *im,* and *them* like *em.*

1 Listen to your teacher read this dialogue.

NEWSPAPER REPORTER: What did A. X. tell Ms. Lyons?

DETECTIVE: He told her that AMBITEL was planning to hire new workers.

NEWSPAPER REPORTER: What did Ms. Lyons tell the police about A. X.?

DETECTIVE: She told them that he didn't care about the workers.

NEWSPAPER REPORTER: What does she want her son to do?

DETECTIVE: She wants him to take over the union. I'm sorry, there's nothing more to say.

2 Repeat the dialogue after your teacher.

3 With a partner, practice the dialogue.

Written Reaction

A. Write five sentences to report your partner's opinions from the OPINION SURVEY on page 56.

Example

Juan doesn't believe that all union leaders are dishonest.

1. _____
2. _____
3. _____
4. _____
5. _____

B. Write a newspaper report about the AMBITEL fire. Mention what you know about the fire, including the cause, the circumstances, the times, the people involved, and the person who started it. Create your own title.

C. Write about your grandfather's (or grandmother's) job. Create your own title.

Unit Ten

Progress?

Reaction

What is progress?
What are some signs of progress?

Interaction

A. A large company is planning to build a new factory in Norwood, a peaceful town located in
green rolling hills. The townspeople are at a town meeting talking about the new factory.
Read some of their comments. Circle + (plus) if the comment is in favor of the new factory
or − (minus) if the comment is against the new factory.

_S_	1. Local Clergyperson:	"We have such a peaceful town now."	+	−
___	2. Housekeeper:	"A new company always raises the standard of living."	+	−
___	3. Sanitation Chief:	"Let's keep our town clean."	+	−
___	4. Parks Director:	"The new factory will help us build a new recreation area."	+	−
___	5. Farmer:	"Crime rates are always higher in industrialized areas."	+	−
___	6. Mayor:	"The town needs the economic boost."	+	−
___	7. Nurse:	"Maybe we'll get better public health service with this factory."	+	−
___	8. Gas Station Operator:	"A new factory helps small businesses in town."	+	−
___	9. Town Council Member:	"The people in this town are good workers."	+	−
___	10. Forest Ranger:	"Industries cause pollution of the environment."	+	−
___	11. Social Worker:	"Unemployment in this area is especially high right now."	+	−
___	12. Restaurant Owner:	"Small towns provide good, honest workers."	+	−
___	13. Dentist:	"People will live better with this new factory here."	+	−
___	14. Police Officer:	"There will probably be an increase in crime."	+	−
___	15. Senior Citizen:	"Public health services improve when new industries move in."	+	−
___	16. Postal Worker:	"Industries should locate in areas where unemployment is high."	+	−
___	17. Insurance Salesperson:	"Industrialization improves the economy."	+	−
___	18. Pharmacist:	"The smaller stores will have more customers."	+	−
___	19. Gym Teacher:	"Better recreational facilities usually result from new industry."	+	−
___	20. Physician:	"More noise and traffic usually are the results of large factories."	+	−

B. Some of the people speak about their feelings in general; others talk about their specific
feelings. Look at the list of comments again. If you feel that the comment is a general one, write
G to the left of it. If you feel that the comment is a specific one, write *S* to the left of it.

C. For each general comment, there is a specific comment expressing almost the same idea. Write
the numbers of the similar comments.

Example

General	Specific
20	1

D. Role play: Work with a partner. Imagine that you are two of the people from part A on page 60. Talk about the plans for the new factory in Norwood.

E. In the following list, which industries would you be in favor of or against if they wanted to locate in your hometown?

1. oil refinery
2. junkyard for used car parts
3. nursery
4. computer chip manufacturer
5. chemical factory
6. textile mill
7. tire factory
8. bakery
9. nuclear power plant
10. coal mine
11. weapons plant
12. mobile home factory

F. In small groups, discuss these questions.

1. Does progress include only new buildings and practices?
2. How does new industry help people? How does it hurt people?
3. What are some things you can do in order to express your feelings about a new factory in your hometown?

Pronunciation   *Have to* and *has to*

In rapid speech, *have to* sounds like *hafta* and *has to* sounds like *hasta*.

1 Listen to your teacher read this dialogue.

TV INTERVIEWER: What does the government have to do?

UNION LEADER: The government has to protect workers.

TV INTERVIEWER: What do the workers have to do?

UNION LEADER: Workers have to speak with one voice.

TV INTERVIEWER: And you provide that voice?

UNION LEADER: We help the workers explain their needs. They don't have to worry.

2 Repeat the dialogue after your teacher.

3 With a partner, practice the dialogue.

Opinion Survey: Progress?

A. Complete the survey. Circle *A* if you agree or *D* if you disagree with the statements.

1. New industries result in better lives for all the people involved.	A	D
2. In developing countries, new industry is the answer.	A	D
3. Industries are leaving developed countries to go to developing countries.	A	D
4. Progress often conflicts with tradition and custom.	A	D
5. Preserving the old is just as important as building the new.	A	D
6. With progress some abuse of workers occurs, but the overall good is worth it.	A	D
7. Industries do not build factories in areas where workers are united.	A	D
8. Industries should pay if they pollute the environment.	A	D
9. American products are better than products made elsewhere.	A	D
10. Foreign countries should preserve their own cultures and environments.	A	D

B. Compare your answers with the other students in your class. Find out how many agree or disagree with the statements. Use numbers to report your class's opinions.

Example

Nine out of ten students agree that new industries result in better lives for all the people involved.

Reading Reaction

A. Before you read this selection, think about these questions.
- What products does the United States export? Import?
- Do you consider it progress for a developing country to imitate American movies, music, computer software, business practices, etc.?

IS THIS PROGRESS?

by M. A. Grant

Not many years ago the United States exported mostly food, weapons, and machinery. Now it exports American entertainment—movies, music, television, books, and computer software. Tom Preston, the president of MTV, stated in the *International Herald Tribune,* "Today's young people have passports to two different worlds—to their own culture and to ours."

(continued)

The spread of American entertainment comes from two worldwide trends: (1) Countries are richer, and (2) people have more free time. Only ten years ago, Hungary did not have any cable television at all. Now 40 percent of Hungarian families can watch CNN or MTV. All over Europe, Asia, and Latin America, people watch films in multiplex theaters, an American-styled group of small theaters together in one building. At the same time, privately owned television stations that show American programs have taken over state-owned monopolies. American culture is also on the newsstand. *Reader's Digest* is published in nineteen languages and has a total of 28 billion readers. Fast-food restaurants are also part of the cultural invasion: McDonald's opens about six new restaurants each day internationally.

Why do people around the world prefer American entertainment? First, U.S. products have a linguistic advantage: They are in English, the first or second language of the developed and developing world. Films in English account for about two-thirds of all films worldwide, most of which are made in the United States. English is also the language of international aviation and computers and the language used in most international meetings. Perhaps another reason for the popularity of American culture is its treatment of American values: respect for the individual, commitment to justice, optimism about the future, making money, and a sense of progress.

Yet some believe that the spread of American culture is an invasion of other cultures and, as a result, a kind of cultural imperialism. It undermines traditional values and encourages evil. America is the Great Satan, and its entertainment products promote not progress, but foolish consumerism, violence, and immorality. Is it progress when a country is losing its cultural soul?

How are language and culture related? Specifically, is American culture a part of the spread of English? Or is English a part of the spread of American culture? It's the chicken-or-the-egg question. Whichever, American entertainment with its sex, speed, and violence sells in most parts of the world.

B. Circle *T* if the statement is true or *F* if the statement is false.

1. People watch CNN and MTV in Eastern Europe.   T   F

2. Developing countries are poorer today.   T   F

3. People do not have as much free time today.   T   F

4. American entertainment includes magazines.   T   F

5. McDonald's is a part of the cultural invasion.   T   F

(continued)

6. An advantage of American entertainment is its use of the native language.   T   F

7. Some believe that the popularity of American entertainment is a kind of cultural imperialism.   T   F

8. Computers have helped in the spread of English.   T   F

C. Answer these questions. Discuss your answers.

1. What were the main American exports years ago?
2. What are the main American exports today?
3. How has American entertainment changed people's lives abroad?
4. What are the reasons that people prefer American entertainment?
5. What are some of the typical American values in films?
6. What is "cultural imperialism"?

Written Reaction

A. Match the words and phrases with their meanings.

1. _g_ (to) boost   a. surroundings, usually referring to natural resources
2. _____ (to) exploit   b. a building where workers make products
3. _____ industrialized   c. (to) use something or someone for one's own good, but not for the good of the thing or person that is used
4. _____ unemployment   d. having a lot of companies/factories
5. _____ recreation   e. maker of a product
6. _____ environment   f. anything done for relaxation in one's free time
7. _____ factory   g. (to) increase in amount or power
8. _____ manufacturer   h. condition of not having a job

B. Use the verbs in parentheses to report eight comments made by the people in part A on page 60.

Example

(say). The local clergyperson said that they had such a peaceful town.

1. (indicate) _____
2. (point out) _____
3. (feel) _____
4. (state) _____
5. (emphasize) _____
6. (assert) _____
7. (claim) _____
8. (believe) _____

C. Write a letter to the editor of the local newspaper, the *Gazette,* and express your feelings regarding the new factory.

D. Write about the values and traditions that are part of your culture that you feel would be important to pass on to future generations. Try to include details on holidays, celebrations, entertainment, and language.

Unit Eleven

Illegal Alien

Reaction

What would a visitor from another planet want to know about us?
What would you want to know about the people on another planet?

Interaction

A. **Read about the situation.**

Shazra is a visitor from a planet called Ostron. Shazra's seat holds her securely. Her space ship, a UFO (Unidentified Flying Object), is going to land on Earth in a short time. It is Shazra's first trip to Earth. Many other Ostrons were here before. Now she has the opportunity to learn for herself. She already knows about PROTRANS (protoplasmic transformation), which allows her to change into a human form. Also, she knows how to speak the most important languages on Earth. Although she is an ET (extraterrestrial), she is able to look and sound like a human being. But there is much more to learn about these people who live on the green planet.

B. **Circle *T* if the statement is true or *F* if the statement is false. If you don't know, circle *?*.**

1. Shazra is in human form in the vehicle.   T   F   ?
2. Shazra was on Earth before.   T   F   ?
3. She is on Earth to learn about humans.   T   F   ?
4. She knows English.   T   F   ?
5. Ostron is in the same solar system as Earth.   T   F   ?
6. Shazra is the first of her kind to visit Earth.   T   F   ?
7. Shazra plans to land her ship at the local airport.   T   F   ?
8. People on Earth are waiting for Shazra's visit.   T   F   ?

C. **Discuss these questions with a partner.**

1. What does Shazra know about humans?
2. Which languages do you think she studied?
3. What do you think Shazra looks like on Ostron?
4. How is she able to look like a human?
5. Which places on Earth will Shazra want to visit?
6. Where will she not be welcome?

D. **Read about the five situations that Shazra sees. In small groups, answer the questions about each situation.**

1. A Dinner Invitation

   Shazra receives an invitation to a dinner party with a family. On Ostron, there is no family unit. Ostronians live in large colonies, like bees or ants, and they eat alone whenever they want.

   • What information about social manners does Shazra need to know?
   • What information about social manners on Ostron do you want to know?

2. Shazra's First Date

A young man wants to go out with Shazra. Shazra is not familiar with dating because young people on Ostron go out in groups.

- What does Shazra need to know about male/female social relations, young people's activities, and the places they often go to?
- What do you want to know about young people on Shazra's planet?

3. Old People

Shazra sees how old people live on Earth. The Ostronians respect their elders, who live a long time. No one is afraid of death, and there is no sadness when someone dies.

- What does Shazra want to know about old people on Earth?
- What information do you want to know about old people on Ostron?

4. Rich and Poor

Shazra notices the economic and social differences among people on Earth. Some are very rich, but many are very poor. On Ostron there is no poverty. Ostronians have what they need, and they share most things.

- What does Shazra want to know about different social classes on Earth?
- What do you want to know about the social organization on Ostron?

5. Education

Children on Ostron do not go to school. Their education is a telepathic process that begins the minute they are born.

- What does Shazra want to know about the educational system on Earth?
- What do you want to know about her educational system?
- What other information would you like to tell Shazra about people on Earth?

Reading Reaction

A. Before reading the selection, think about these questions.

- Some people believe in UFOs. Do you think they are crazy?
- What are some explanations for UFOs?

Incident at Midnight

by Freddy Katz

It was just after midnight. I was driving home from work after an eight-hour shift. I'm a security guard at the Potato Hill nuclear plant. The night was very foggy, and I had to drive slowly. I kept looking to the right so I could make out the edge of the road in the fog.

Just as I was going over a hill, I noticed that there were lights around me. My old truck was gasping to get up the hill. Once over the hill, it died. The motor stopped, and I coasted to the bottom, where the railroad track is. Not many trains use the railroad anymore—only an occasional freight train. Then I noticed that the light was no longer coming from around me but was off to the side—bright and shining right into the truck. It lit up the entire inside. I tried to start the motor. There was no reaction at all when I stepped on the starter. Using only the starter, I was able to move the truck so that it cleared the track. I heard a loud roar. I don't remember much about what happened next.

(continued)

The light seemed to embrace me, and the entire truck started to shake. I quickly got out of the truck and ran to the grass beside the road. They found me there the next morning. I don't know what happened during those six or so hours. Each day, however, I remember something more. I recall some sort of spaceship and strange little people around me. They didn't speak as they examined me. They seemed to communicate with me by thoughts.

Whatever happened to me that night is still a mystery, but some other people in this area have reported similar experiences. Most of them think they had an incident with a UFO. This is my first time to talk about this with anyone. I don't want people to think I'm crazy.

B. Circle *T* if the statement is true or *F* if the statement is false. If you don't know, circle *?*.

1. The writer was in his truck.   T   F   ?
2. The writer is a man.   T   F   ?
3. The writer stopped his car to look at the light.   T   F   ?
4. The writer slept in his truck all night.   T   F   ?
5. The writer had an incident with a UFO.   T   F   ?
6. The night was clear.   T   F   ?
7. The writer remembers everything that happened.   T   F   ?
8. No one else believes what happened to this man.   T   F   ?

C. Answer these questions. Discuss your answers with a partner.

1. When did the writer go to work? Get off work? Wake up?
2. What was the first indication that something strange was happening?
3. What did the man see? What did he hear? What did he feel?
4. What are some of the things that he remembered later?
5. Why didn't he tell someone about this incident sooner?
6. What is a logical explanation for this incident?
7. What questions do you want to ask this man?

Opinion Survey: UFOs and Aliens

A. Complete the survey. Circle *A* if you agree or *D* if you disagree with the statements.

	A	D
1. UFOs are real.	A	D
2. The government knows that UFOs exist, but they keep it a secret.	A	D
3. People who have seen UFOs are probably a little crazy.	A	D
4. Although I haven't seen a UFO, it's possible that they exist.	A	D
5. We are not alone in the universe.	A	D
6. There is usually an explanation for a UFO.	A	D
7. Beings from other planets have probably visited Earth.	A	D
8. There are other life-forms in the universe.	A	D
9. Science and technology on Earth are probably not equal to those of other planets with life.	A	D
10. People on Earth are not ready for aliens from another planet.	A	D

B. Compare your answers with the other students' answers. Find out how many agree with the statements. Then, with a partner, ask each other questions about your class's opinions. In your answers use expressions such as: *none, not many, a few, several, many, most,* and *all.*

Example

STUDENT A: How does the class feel about UFOs?

STUDENT B: Most of the students feel that UFOs are real even if they haven't seen one. How does the class feel about people who have seen UFOs?

STUDENT A: A few of them feel they are crazy.

Pronunciation Acronyms

An acronym is a word formed by using the first letters of each word in a group of words. We pronounce some acronyms by saying the letters individually—for example, USA, for the United States of America. We pronounce other acronyms like words—for example, NATO, for North Atlantic Treaty Organization.

1 Listen to your teacher read these acronyms.

	Acronym	Pronounced Like a Word
a.	USA (U)nited (S)tates of (A)merica	
b.	NATO (N)orth (A)tlantic (T)reaty (O)rganization	X
c.	SCUBA (S)elf-(C)ontained (U)nderwater (B)reathing (A)pparatus	
d.	NASA (N)ational (A)eronautics and (S)pace (A)dministration	
e.	MTV (M)usic (T)ele(v)ision	
f.	CNN (C)able (N)etwork (N)ews	
g.	ASAP (A)s (Soon) (A)s (P)ossible	
h.	AIDS (A)cquired (I)mmune (D)eficiency (S)yndrome	
i.	UN (U)nited (N)ations	
j.	NAFTA (N)orth (A)merican (F)ree (T)rade (A)greement	
k.	IBM (I)nternational (B)usiness (M)achines	
l.	CIA (C)entral (I)ntelligence (A)gency	
m.	ROM (R)ead (O)nly (M)emory	
n.	LASER (L)ight (A)mplification by (S)imulated (E)mission of (R)adiation	

2 Listen again. Place an X next to those that are pronounced like words.

3 Repeat the acronyms after your teacher.

4 With a partner, practice saying the acronyms.

Written Reaction

A. Match the words and phrases with their meanings.

   _b_   1. (to) land   a. sending and receiving messages through the mind

        2. (to) go out with someone   b. (to) touch the ground after a flight

        3. colony   c. (to) honor older people

        4. dating   d. (to) give some of what you have to other people

        5. (to) respect elders   e. condition of having very little money or belongings

        6. poverty   f. spending time with someone you like romantically on a regular basis

        7. (to) share   g. group of individuals living and working together

        8. telepathy   h. (to) go to the movies, dinner, etc., with a friend or romantic interest

B. Write four things that Shazra needs to know about the social, educational, or economic conditions of people on Earth.

Example

It is appropriate to bring a gift to the host of a dinner party.

1. _____

2. _____

3. _____

4. _____

C. Write four things you know about Shazra's life on Ostron.

Example

On Ostron there is no public educational system.

1. _____

2. _____

3. _____

4. _____

D. Write a paragraph about a strange incident you had. Look back at the reading on pages 69–70 as an example.

Unit Twelve

Energy Crisis

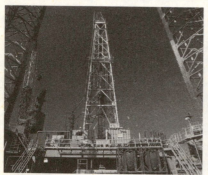
oil wells

solar panels

nuclear power plant

hydroelectric dam

wind-powered propellers

natural gas pipeline

Reaction

What do these pictures show?

Which kinds of energy are you most familiar with?

Interaction

A. Match the kind of energy with its description. Compare your answers with a partner.

   _f_   1. petroleum products

         2. solar power

         3. thermonuclear power

         4. hydroelectric power

         5. wind power

         6. natural gas

a. comes from dams built on rivers or other bodies of water

b. comes from the heat of the sun

c. comes from underground and is moved through pipes

d. is produced by splitting atoms

e. is generated by huge propellers in open places

f. includes gas and oil for cars, planes, heating, etc.

B. The Seneca Oil Company operates two oil wells, Oyster Bay and Zuma Field. The company is going to expand one of these wells. Study the information in the table, and answer the questions. Discuss your answers with a partner.

1. Which well is cheaper to operate?

2. Which one has better facilities for its workers?

3. Which one should be expanded?

4. Would you be concerned if you lived near Zuma Field? Near Oyster Bay?

5. In what ways can these oil wells cause pollution?

6. How could oil companies reduce pollution from these wells?

	Oyster Bay Well	Zuma Field Well
Location	24 km (15 mi) offshore	12 km (7 1/2 mi) from town
Number of Employees	8	7
Nearest Settlement	small fishing village (population: 800) near popular beach	large agricultural/oil city (population: 500,000)
Method of Transporting Crude Oil	two-day tanker trip	one day through pipeline
Quality of Oil	average quality expensive to refine	excellent quality refining not so costly
Living Conditions for Workers	crowded living space on rig; workers must stay at least a week without families	comfortable homes in city; workers live at home with families and commute daily

C. Discuss these questions with a partner.

Which kind of energy

1. is the most dangerous? Why?
2. is the most expensive at the present time? The cheapest?
3. is the oldest? The newest?
4. significantly changes the environment?
5. is probably the most used around the world?
6. is probably the cleanest? The dirtiest?

D. Discuss these questions about the various kinds of energy in the world today.

1. What are some ways that energy is wasted today in automobiles, in home heating/cooling, in lighting, or in electrical appliances/machinery?
2. Which alternative sources of energy need developing? Why?
3. Which kinds of energy should be stopped or limited? Why?
4. Which kinds of energy will people probably use in the future?
5. Which countries use the various kinds of energy on the list in part A on page 75?
6. Should a country or company that has an important product charge high prices for it?
7. What arrangements are necessary so that all countries can have the energy they need?

Opinion Survey: Energy and the Environment

A. Complete the survey. Circle *A* if you agree or *D* if you disagree with the statements.

1. There is an energy crisis in the world today.	A	D
2. Countries have to share their energy sources.	A	D
3. Some countries have to decrease their use of energy.	A	D
4. If we use less energy, no other energy sources are needed.	A	D
5. Using more energy is necessary if we are to make progress.	A	D
6. Each country has to develop and use its own energy sources.	A	D
7. Every type of energy source has some disadvantage.	A	D
8. Scientists will discover many new energy sources in the future.	A	D
9. Having enough energy is more important than protecting the environment.	A	D
10. Energy will probably get more expensive.	A	D

B. Compare your answers with the other students in your class. Find out the percentage of students who agree or disagree with the statements.

Example

Fifty percent of the students in this class think that there is an energy crisis in the world today.

Reading Reaction

A. Before reading the selection, think about these questions.
- Which forms of energy are most used today?
- Which forms of energy will people use in the future?

ENERGY FOR THE FUTURE

by Tern F. Dalite

Is there really an energy crisis? Or do we depend too much on a single form of energy? During recent generations, the world depended mostly on hydroelectric power. Governments built dams across rivers, forming large lakes and putting thousands of acres of land under water. The water flowing over the dams turned turbines to generate electricity. Today giant power lines carry electricity to distant cities. Some scientists say that these power lines are dangerous because of the electromagnetic fields they produce. More and more people object to hydroelectric power because it seriously changes the balance of nature.

Thermonuclear power, or nuclear power, comes from the splitting of atoms. It is a widely used and inexpensive form of energy. However, it is possibly the most dangerous because there are health risks from radiation.

Coal, one type of fossil fuel, is one of the dirtiest kinds of energy used. It heats homes and runs factories. Other fossil fuels that come from the earth are petroleum products: gasoline, which is used for most vehicles, and natural gas, which is used for some vehicles, but mostly for heating and cooking. At the present time, some New York City buses run on natural gas, which is cleaner and cheaper than regular gasoline.

Alcohol is quite commonly used as fuel in Brazil. It comes from one of Brazil's main crops, sugar cane, which is easily processed into alcohol. Methane gas, another source of fuel, comes from garbage, but it is not widely used. From under the ground, Iceland gets geothermal energy, which provides most of the country's heat and hot water. Other sources of energy include the wind and the sun. In Hawaii, for example, the strong winds in some locations turn giant propellers to produce electricity. In many parts of the world the sun fulfills many energy needs. Solar panels heated by the sun produce electricity. Solar energy already provides many homes with heat and hot water.

(continued)

What about future sources of energy? Ralph Hansen, a NASA engineer and the author of *Sun Power,* proposed a plan to use solar-powered satellites to capture the power of the sun in space, where the sun shines 24 hours a day, 365 days a year. His plan would provide low-cost, nonpolluting energy for the entire world. An additional energy source to be developed is fusion energy, the process that powers the sun and the stars. Nuclear fusion, or fusion, represents an unlimited source of energy. In fusion, nuclei combine to form bigger nuclei while releasing energy. Not much is known about how to make it usable, but it seems promising, and millions of dollars of government money will help develop it. Although these sources of energy seem easily available, their high cost is a problem. They are expensive to develop. As a result, they are not as widely used as cheaper forms of fuel.

Energy is needed to warm us, cool us, light our way, carry us from one place to another, and process our food. If the world population increases as expected, resources for the kinds of energy we use today may be insufficient. We will have to look closer at different energy sources, such as fusion and solar power. When will we decide to spend the money necessary to develop these energy sources? Who will pay for it? These questions will need to be answered before we can meet our growing energy needs.

B. Circle the correct answers. Some sentences have more than one correct answer.

1. Fossil fuels include (nuclear energy / hydroelectric power / petroleum / coal).
2. (Nuclear energy / Fossil fuel / Alcohol / Hydroelectric power) is dangerous because of radiation.
3. In some places vehicles use (gasoline / coal / alcohol / natural gas).
4. Natural sources of energy come from (wind / sun / water / fusion).
5. Hansen suggests getting energy from (wind / fusion / sun / garbage).
6. Iceland is famous for its (nuclear / coal / geothermal / solar) power.
7. The problem with most alternative sources of energy is: (The technology is not ready. / The costs are too high. / They are dangerous. / They are limited.)
8. (Geothermal energy / Nuclear energy / Solar power / Hydroelectric power) comes from splitting atomic particles.

C. Answer these questions. Discuss your answers.

1. Where are the various forms of energy used?
2. What materials are necessary to produce each form of energy?
3. What technology is necessary for each form of energy?
4. Where does each form of energy exist?
5. What sorts of energy will the future produce?
6. What is your answer to the energy crisis?

Pronunciation Stress in Superlatives

In a phrase including a superlative, the stressed syllable in the adjective usually receives the strongest stress in the phrase. For example, *dan* in *dangerous* receives the strongest stress in the phrase "the most dangerous form of energy."

1 Listen to your teacher read these superlative adjective phrases. Circle the stressed syllable in each phrase.

a. the most dangerous form of energy

b. the newest form of energy

c. the costliest form of energy

d. the dirtiest form of energy

e. the most expensive form of energy

f. the cleanest form of energy

g. the cheapest form of energy

h. the most reliable form of energy

i. the most plentiful form of energy

2 Repeat the phrases after your teacher.

3 With a partner, ask and answer questions about the different forms of energy.

Written Reaction

A. Complete the blanks with the correct noun or verb. Use your dictionary if necessary.

Verb

1. (to) pollute the environment

2. (to) refine petroleum

3. (to) commute to work

4. (to) eliminate our dependence on one fuel

5. (to) _____

6. (to) _____

7. (to) _____ their homes

Noun

environmental _____

petroleum _____

_____

_____

dependence on fossil fuels

generation of clean energy

heat/heating (for their homes)

B. Write your opinion of each kind of energy. Use complete sentences.

Example

Hydroelectric power: Hydroelectric power is the most used energy in the world, but I am against using this kind of energy and changing the balance of nature.

1. Nuclear energy: _____

2. Coal: _____

3. Petroleum: _____

4. Solar energy: _____

5. Wind power: _____

6. Natural gas: _____

7. Alcohol: _____

8. Geothermal energy: _____

C. Write an editorial for the newspaper. Decide if you are in favor of or opposed to a specific kind of energy and explain why.

Unit Thirteen

Those Golden Years

Reaction

Do these retired Americans seem different from retired people in your country?
How are they different? How are they similar?

Interaction

A. Read the following conversation between Lydia and Edgar. They are an older couple, and they are discussing their retirement.

LYDIA: All these brochures! I don't know what to do. Where are we going to retire? I'm confused.

EDGAR: Why don't we just stay here in the city?

LYDIA: We don't need this large apartment.

EDGAR: I suppose you're right. Let's think of other places.

LYDIA: Besides, a big city is not a good place to grow old.

EDGAR: How about some place nearer the kids?

LYDIA: I'm not sure that's a good idea. I don't want to spend my retirement babysitting.

EDGAR: Mmmm, I don't either. We can go to different places and do different things.

LYDIA: Yes, that's the spirit. But at our own pace.

EDGAR: Maybe even someplace abroad.

LYDIA: Yeah, we both speak Spanish.

EDGAR: Hey, this retirement thing is exciting. Let me take a look at those brochures.

B. Circle *T* if the statement is true or *F* if the statement is false. Compare your answers with a partner.

1. Lydia and Edgar are probably going to retire soon.	T	F
2. They want to be near their children.	T	F
3. They want to stay in the city.	T	F
4. They probably do not want a slower pace.	T	F
5. Lydia wants to spend more time with her grandchildren.	T	F
6. Edgar becomes enthusiastic about retirement.	T	F
7. Lydia and Edgar speak another language.	T	F
8. They are not interested in living outside the United States.	T	F

C. Answer these questions. Discuss your answers with a partner.

1. Approximately how old are Lydia and Edgar?
2. Where do they live now?
3. How do they feel about living near their children?
4. How do they feel about their retirement?
5. How do they feel about living outside the United States?

D. Answer these questions. Discuss your answers with a partner.

1. What are some advantages and disadvantages of retirement?
2. What questions does one need to ask when retiring to a different location?
3. What are the needs of retired people? What would be the best choices for them from each category?

Climate	Environment	Activities	Housing	Social Companions
dry	large city	gambling	high-rise apartment	people their own age
hot	small town	swimming	house	children
sunny	suburb	skiing	retirement community	grandchildren
cold	middle-sized city	dancing	nursing home	mixed ages
rainy	the country	museums	with children	alone
humid	abroad	concerts		

E. Read the charts and decide where Edgar and Lydia should retire. Discuss your decision with a partner.

	Tropical Isle	Mountain Glen	Pinos Placidos	New York City
Climate	humid, sunny, hot all year; little rain but usually floods	sunny and rainy days; beautiful fall; snow/ice in winter; cool spring/summer; four seasons	hot, dry summer; three seasons; one rainy season	four seasons; hot summers; cold, snowy, icy winters
Environment	well-to-do pensioners; active nightlife; near city/cultural events; not so safe	most retirees spend only three seasons there; near medium-sized city; very safe	in Central America; Spanish-speaking; friendly atmosphere; friends there; quite safe	many friends; familiar with the fast lifestyle; dangerous for seniors; the Big Apple
Activities	boating, swimming, beach, gambling	swimming pool, skiing, hiking, mountain climbing; bird watching	very few social activities; have to make your own; can work part-time (teaching)	a cultural paradise (museums, shows, concerts, libraries), free or reduced for seniors; can work part-time

	Tropical Isle	Mountain Glen	Pinos Placidos	New York City
Economy	expensive, must use savings as well as pension; special services for retirees	relatively inexpensive; could afford a servant on their pension alone	very cheap; luxurious living conditions; two servants possible on pension; travel costly because of distance	very expensive; no servants; easy to travel from various airports
Health Conditions	no food precautions necessary; medicine and doctors plentiful	no health precautions other than the cold in winter; medical facilities in the next city	food/water precautions needed; medications available cheaply	known doctors and medical facilities; no health precautions; reliable social services
Housing	high-rise apartment near the water; no space for visitors	medium-sized villa with patio and garden; room for children but far away from them	luxurious condo on the ocean; private garden/pool; gardener; plenty of space for visitors	have to move to a smaller apartment with limited services and no space for visitors

F. Role Play: Work with a partner. Student A: Imagine that you are Lydia and Edgar's son or daughter. What advice do you have for your parents? Try to persuade one of your parents to agree with you. Student B: Imagine that you are Lydia or Edgar. Where do you want to retire? Explain to your son or daughter where you want to retire and why.

G. In a small group, discuss these questions.
- When will you retire?
- Where will you retire?
- What will you do in retirement?

Opinion Survey: Aging and Retirement

A. Complete the survey. Circle *A* if you agree or *D* if you disagree with the statements.

1. It is necessary for people to retire at a certain age.	**A**	**D**
2. Families have to take care of very old family members.	**A**	**D**
3. Older workers are more patient than younger workers.	**A**	**D**
4. Older people have physical limitations.	**A**	**D**
5. Young workers have an obligation to pay for older people's retirement benefits.	**A**	**D**
6. It is better for aging parents to live with their children.	**A**	**D**
7. Physical exercise is unsuitable for older people.	**A**	**D**
8. It is best for older people to stay in retirement homes.	**A**	**D**
9. Old people need to be with young people.	**A**	**D**
10. Young people can learn from older people.	**A**	**D**

B. Compare your answers with a partner. Report your answers and your partner's answers to the class using expressions such as *both, neither,* and *but.*

Examples

Neither Amelia nor I think that people need to retire at a certain age.

Enrique thinks people need to retire at a certain age, but I disagree.

Reading Reaction

A. Before reading the selection, think about these questions.
- What role do you think stress plays in getting older?
- What role does science play in helping people grow older?

The Best Is Yet to Be

by Elder Leigh

A French woman, Jeanne Calment, lived to the ripe old age of 122—longer than any other person on earth. She was born in 1875 and died in 1997. Other people said they were older, but they did not have legal papers to prove it. A few years before Mrs. Calment died, she said, "I see badly, I hear badly, I can't feel anything, but everything's fine." Many old people have the same problems. However, in the future, according to scientists, a person of

(continued)

Mrs. Calment's age will not be so unusual. Scientists are beginning to find out more about the secrets of aging. The time from birth to death for a human ". . . is not a fixed process," says Dr. Michael Rose, a biologist from the University of California. Dr. Rose says about aging, "It's nothing fixed; it's nothing absolute; it's nothing preset from the day you're born." Aging is not fixed like the colors of a bird's feathers, which depend on genetics. Scientists now talk about 150-year-olds and 200-year-olds. Our children in the twenty-first century will probably live to these ages.

Aging is different from growing older, and there are many factors that influence aging. On the Savannah River in Georgia, Dr. Whitfield Gibbons studied turtles to see why they grow older but do not appear to age. They reproduce until death. Opossums that live on a Georgia island, where there are no predators, do not age as fast as opossums on the mainland, where there are predators. Aging, then, is related in some way to stress in the environment. In that regard, Mrs. Calment apparently found the secret. In spite of her aches and pains, "everything's fine." She knew how to deal with stress.

We also know that diet is important as one grows older—not only what we eat but how much. Some scientists believe that less is better. Fewer calories increase one's life. Also, exercise is important. Dr. Miriam Nelson, of Tufts University, discovered that exercise, even a little bit, turns back the clock for elderly people. They regain muscle tone—even people in their 90s. Needless to say, bad habits are hard to break. Excessive drinking and smoking will hurt you and will cause you to age faster. People who smoke, for example, develop facial wrinkles more quickly.

Keeping busy is another way to prevent aging. Angeline Strandahl cooked every day for her two children, a 67-year-old daughter and a 69-year-old son, until her death at the age of 104. People feel better about themselves if they are useful and appreciated.

So, if you want to live to a ripe old age, eat less, exercise more, avoid stress, make yourself useful, and avoid bad habits. Also, don't get hit by a truck.

B. Match the following sentence parts.

   h   1. Angeline Strandahl   a. is not fixed or preset.

        2. Jeanne Calment   b. can increase one's life span.

        3. Consuming fewer calories   c. restores muscles in elderly people.

        4. Turtles in Georgia   d. people will live to be over 150 years old.

        5. Opossums in Georgia   e. show differences in aging related to stress.

        6. In the future scientists say that   f. grow older but do not seem to age.

        7. Even a little bit of exercise   g. probably lived longer than any other person on earth.

        8. The range from birth to death   h. cooked every day for her children until her death.

C. Answer these questions. Discuss your answers with a partner.

1. Why was Mrs. Calment famous?
2. What was her attitude toward life?
3. What does the biologist from California say about aging?
4. What is the difference between aging and growing older?
5. What factors influence aging?
6. What do the studies of turtles and opossums show about aging?
7. In terms of aging, what is important about one's diet? Exercise? Stress? Bad habits? Feeling useful?
8. How do you feel about aging? Is the best yet to be?

Pronunciation **Stress and Intonation in Adjective Phrases**

Notice how the stress and intonation change in these adjective phrases: _22 years old,_ a _22-year-old woman._

1 Listen to your teacher read these sentences. Underline the syllables that are stressed and circle the part of the sentence where your voice rises.

a. Mrs. Calment was 122 years old.	She was a 122-year-old woman.
b. Mrs. Strandahl was 104 years old.	She was a 104-year-old woman.
c. Her son was 69 years old.	He was a 69-year-old man.
d. Her grandson is 4 months old.	He is a 4-month-old boy.
e. This bread is 3 weeks old.	This is 3-week-old bread.
f. This e-mail message is 5 days old.	This is a 5-day-old e-mail message.

2 Repeat the sentences after your teacher.

3 With a partner, practice saying the sentences using the correct stress and intonation.

Written Reaction

A. Complete the paragraph. Use the words or phrases in the box.

physical	wrinkles	to retire	stress
climate	elderly	aging	

Many _____ people want to travel after retirement. Others prefer to stay in one place.
  1.

Some like to live in a warm _____. My grandfather was like that. He wanted _____ in
  2.   3.

Florida. He did not have any serious _____ limitations, and the only exercise he got was
  4.

walking, which seemed to be great for him. His mind was always alert. His skin was smooth;

he had very few _____ on his face. Nothing worried him, so he had very little _____ in his
  5.   6.

life. "Everything's O.K.," he always said. He liked to do things for other people. He always

looked younger than he was. He lived to be 97, which was only a number to him. He felt

that _____ is not an absolute process. One grows older, but one doesn't have to age. He had
  7.

a very good attitude about the future. "The best is yet to be," he always said.

B. Where do you want to retire? Choose a place to retire and write four sentences about why you would like to retire there.

Example

I want to retire in Brazil. It has a warm, tropical climate. I have been there many times, and the people are friendly. It's also inexpensive to live there.

1. _____
2. _____
3. _____
4. _____

C. Where do you *not* want to retire? Write four sentences about this place.

Example

I don't want to retire in New York City because it is expensive and noisy.

1. _____
2. _____
3. _____
4. _____

D. Write a paragraph about an elderly person. Create your own title. Talk about some of the following topics: his/her daily routine, exercise habits, attitude toward stress, age, diet, desire to be useful.

A Home for Little Sarah

Reaction

What are some factors in adopting a baby?

Do adopted children have the right to know who their biological parents are?

Interaction

A. The name of the little girl in the photo on page 88 is Sarah, and she needs a home. Here are the six candidates who applied to the Family Makers Adoption Agency. They all want to adopt a baby. Read about them.

1.

NAME: Charles and Emily Hudson

ADDRESS: 45 Valley Road,
Apartment 10C
San Diego, CA 92124

STATEMENT: We want a baby so much, but we can't have one. Right now I am working as a plumber's assistant and Emily as a waitress. We are working hard to save money so we can get a house of our own and give our adopted child the things that he or she will need. We both like to have a good time, but we are ready for a baby to help us settle down.

Would you consider interracial adoption? Yes.

2.

NAME: Pedron and Ofelia Jimenez

ADDRESS: 344 Opalaka Road
Miami, Florida 33133

STATEMENT: Although we don't have a lot of money, we both love kids. My wife is a full-time mother and housewife, and I am an elementary school teacher. We already have three adopted children, and it's no problem to fit another one into our family. Six people can live as cheaply as five.

Would you consider interracial adoption? Yes.

3.

NAME: Jennifer Hamilton

ADDRESS: 679 Park Avenue
New York, NY 10021

STATEMENT: I am a successful lawyer. I have always wanted to be a mother, but I have not found the right partner. There are a lot of successful single mothers raising children.

Would you consider interracial adoption? No, I want an African American baby, someone I can identify with.

4.

NAME: Dr. Paul and Dr. Lila Chan

ADDRESS: 250 28 Street, NW
Georgetown, DC 20007

STATEMENT: We both have spent years studying. Now we have good positions—I'm a surgeon and my husband is a dentist—and we would like to adopt a baby to fit into our family. We just don't have time to have a baby ourselves and there are so many children who need homes.

Would you consider interracial adoption? Yes, if necessary.

5.

NAME: Mr. Oscar Fields

ADDRESS: 9 Freeman Drive
Kansas City, MO 64141

STATEMENT: I love children, but I don't want to get married again. I know how to take care of a baby because I took care of my younger brothers and sisters. My job as a computer programmer/consultant allows me to work at home a lot so I can be with the baby myself.

Would you consider interracial adoption? I would prefer an African American baby.

6.

Family Makers

Adoption Agency

NAME: Mr. J. Seth and Eileen Gold

ADDRESS: 27 Cowhide Drive
Dallas, TX 75266

STATEMENT: We tried to have children, but modern science has not helped us. My wife, a former "Miss Dallas," has a lot of time to care for the child. So we want to adopt a child who will be the heir to my oil company.

Would you consider interracial adoption?   Yes, but we prefer a baby like us.

B. Answer these questions with a partner.

Which of the candidates

1. is the richest?
2. is the poorest?
3. is single?
4. has other children?
5. can't have their own children?
6. is willing to adopt an African American baby?
7. is not enthusiastic about adopting an African American baby?
8. only wants an African American baby?
9. is the least qualified?
10. is the most qualified?

C. Decide who should adopt Sarah. Discuss these questions.

1. Does it matter that Sarah is African American?
2. Does it matter that Sarah is a little girl?
3. Does it matter that some of the candidates are not African American?
4. Does the race of the parents matter?
5. Is it important for Sarah to have brothers and sisters?
6. Is it important for Sarah to have two parents?

Reading Reaction

A. Before reading the selection, think about these questions.

- What are your feelings about interracial adoption?
- What are some of the issues regarding interracial adoption?

Interracial Adoption

by Sarah Gate

For Michael and Rose Gardner, a white couple, it seems so simple. They want to give a home to Gerald, a black baby, who needs one. Unfortunately, it is not so simple because of the feelings about interracial adoption. Some social workers believe that adoptions between races—particularly between white parents and black children—are harmful. Such adoptions, they say, deny the children their cultural heritage. These children may later experience an identity crisis. They will not know exactly who they are. Also, children from interracial adoptive families may develop low self-esteem and a feeling of insecurity around other children. Most experts agree that matching the racial and ethnic backgrounds of children to their adoptive parents is preferable. However, in the United States, many minority children need parents, and there just aren't enough minority parents to adopt them.

Helen Byers is a successful black architect who lived in a white family when she was a child. "My adoptive parents were good to me," she said. "But I have difficulty relating to other blacks. Even little things like my appearance. I'm not sure about how to fix my hair and identify as African American. I went to all-white schools. My friends were all white. I did not really socialize with any people of my own race," she pointed out. "Don't get me wrong. I love my adoptive mother and father and my brothers and sisters. They gave me a wonderful home and a good education. I am grateful for that, but I'm just now beginning to find out exactly who I am. Fortunately, my adoptive family understands this."

B. Circle *T* if the statement is true or *F* if the statement is false.

1. Interracial adoption is one solution for many black children who need homes.   T   F

2. Some social workers are opposed to interracial adoptions.   T   F

3. The architect had a good sense of her black background.   T   F

4. The couple think it is a simple matter to adopt Gerald.   T   F

5. Interracial adoptions always give a child higher self-esteem than same-race adoptions.   T   F

6. Most experts agree that interracial adoption is best.   T   F

C. Answer these questions. Discuss your answers with a partner.

1. How does the couple feel about adopting a black baby?
2. How do some social workers feel about interracial adoption?
3. How does the architect feel about her childhood?
4. How does she feel now toward other black people?
5. How does her adoptive family feel about her attempt to identify with her African heritage?

D. Read the following classified ad. Answer the questions.

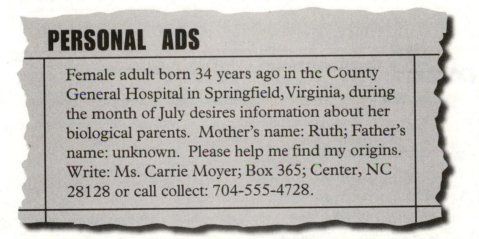

PERSONAL ADS

Female adult born 34 years ago in the County General Hospital in Springfield, Virginia, during the month of July desires information about her biological parents. Mother's name: Ruth; Father's name: unknown. Please help me find my origins. Write: Ms. Carrie Moyer; Box 365; Center, NC 28128 or call collect: 704-555-4728.

1. Why did this person place this ad in the newspaper?
2. What are some possible reasons for her adoption?
3. How do you think her adoptive parents feel about her search for her biological parents?
4. Carrie Moyer plans to have children. Why is her biological background important?

Opinion Survey: Adoption

A. Complete the survey. Circle *A* if you agree or *D* if you disagree with the statements.

1. Adoptive children have a right to see their adoption records.   A   D
2. It's better if a minority child is adopted by members of the same minority.   A   D
3. Love, not money, is most important in adoption.   A   D
4. It's better if an adoptive child is in a family with other children.   A   D
5. It's better if a married couple adopts a child.   A   D
6. It's more difficult to adopt an older child.   A   D
7. If an adoption doesn't work out, the adoptive parents have to return the child.   A   D
8. Adoption is for those couples who cannot have children of their own.   A   D

B. Compare your answers with a partner. Then, in a group, report your answer to each item. Use *and* or *but* to compare your answers.

Examples

I think adoptive children have a right to see their adoption records, and Ari thinks so too.
I think adoptive children have a right to see their adoption records, but Yukiko doesn't think so.

Pronunciation · Contractions with *would*

When *would* is contracted with a pronoun, it sounds like *d*. When *would* is contracted with *not*, it sounds like *wu-n*. Remember: Do not contract *would* with a pronoun in short negative answers.

1 Listen to your teacher read this dialogue.

MARIA: Would you consider adopting a child?

MAXINE: Yes, I would. I'd like to do that. How about you?

MARIA: No, I wouldn't. I wouldn't want to because sometimes those children have problems and I wouldn't feel able to help them.

MAXINE: Would you adopt an infant?

MARIA: Maybe. Would you consider adopting a child with a physical disability?

MAXINE: Sure. I'd do that.

2 Repeat the dialogue after your teacher.

3 With a partner, practice the dialogue between Maria and Maxine.

Written Reaction

A. Complete the sentences. Use the phrases in the box.

cultural heritage	identity crisis	low self-esteem
adoptive parent	biological parent	

1. The background of one's family over several generations is one's _____ .

2. People who are confused about who they are have an _____ .

3. A person without self-respect has _____ .

4. The woman who gave birth to you is your _____ .

5. After a legal process of taking a child into your family, you are the child's _____ .

B. Write three reasons for or against interracial adoption.

Example

Interracial adoption is a way for minority children who need a home to have one.

1. _____

2. _____

3. _____

C. Write three sentences for or against adopted children seeing their adoption records.

Example

Adopted adults need to see their adoption records for health reasons.

1. _____

2. _____

3. _____

D. Write an editorial for a newspaper *for* or *against* interracial adoption. Write your own title for the editorial.

Life

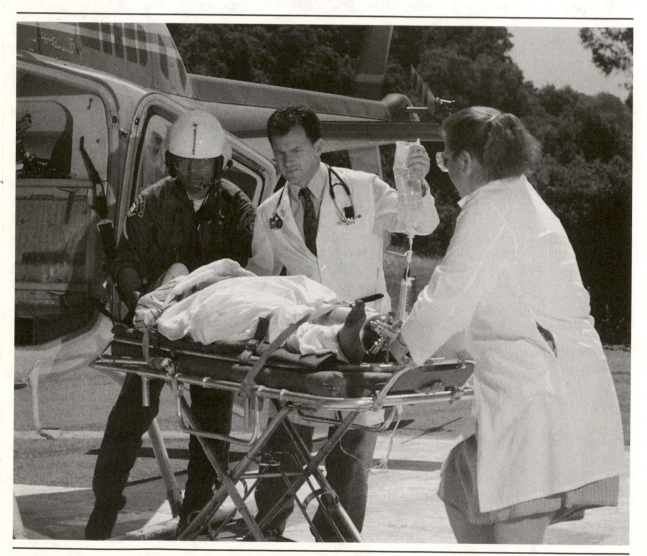

Reaction

- How do you feel about artificial life support?
- When exactly does death occur?

Interaction

A. Read the following reports.

> **July 17:** Tampa—A Rainbow Airlines plane crashed on landing at the local airport. There were several survivors, and they were taken to a nearby hospital.

> **July 18:** Among the survivors of yesterday's Rainbow Airlines crash are Mrs. Grace Hernandez, 46, and her daughter, Juanita, 18. Both are in serious condition.

> **July 19:** Mrs. Hernandez and her daughter are still unconscious and are not expected to live. Their survival so far has amazed the medical experts and their family.

> **July 27:** Mrs. Hernandez and her daughter Juanita, survivors of the Rainbow Airlines crash, are now in guarded but stable condition. Neither has woken up since the crash. Life-support systems are keeping them alive, but their doctors have little hope that they will ever get better.

> **December 20:** Over five months have passed since the two crash survivors were put on life-support machines. Doctors are puzzled by the patients' conditions.

B. In a small group, discuss the situations.

1. The husband and father, Mr. Luis Hernandez, wants the life-support machines disconnected, but the doctors refuse. Why does Mr. Hernandez want them disconnected? Why do the doctors refuse to disconnect the patients?

2. Suppose Mr. Hernandez wants both his wife and daughter to remain on the life-support machines. However, he has to pay for this care and he has enough money for only one machine. Which person should continue on the life-support machine—his wife or his daughter?

3. After waiting a long time for his wife and daughter to wake up, Mr. Hernandez feels that they are no longer living a normal, full life and should be helped to die. The practice of helping someone die is called euthanasia. Why do you think euthanasia is illegal in many countries? Should Mr. Hernandez be able to help his wife and daughter die?

C. Role Play: Work with a partner. Imagine that you are Mr. Hernandez and the doctor. Discuss the pros and cons of life support and come to an agreement.

D. In a small group, discuss the following.

1. List as many reasons as possible why doctors *should* use life-support machines. Compare your list with other students' lists.

2. List as many reasons as possible why doctors *should not* use life-support machines. Compare your list with other students' lists.

3. If you think doctors should use life-support systems, should they use them:

   a. indefinitely or only for a certain period of time?

   b. on patients with terminal diseases or temporary illness?

   c. with or without the approval of the patient's family?

   d. on patients who have no money or insurance?

   e. on patients who are in a vegetative state?

   f. on patients who are in great pain?

   g. on elderly patients?

Reading Reaction

A. Before reading the selection, think about these questions.

- Is it O.K. to help a loved one die?
- What is a doctor's role in caring for terminally ill people?

DR. DEATH

by Marcy N. Kighness

He's a simple man, who has only one suit. It's the dark-colored conservative one that he wears to his trials. Usually he wears a shirt and tie and in the winter a blue sweater. He lives alone. His small home is comfortable but not luxurious. His hobby is playing his electric organ. He's a retired pathologist, almost 75 years old, and has the gentle look of a thin and frail uncle. It's hard to believe that this man is Dr. Death. He's Dr. Jack Kevorkian, one of the most controversial men in the United States today.

Why is he so controversial? Because he helps people die. Some people say that he plays God by doing this. Others feel that he has great sympathy for the terminally ill. He helps only those who ask to die. In doing this, he has broken some laws, but he feels that he is doing a greater good. "Pass any law you want," he says, " It will not stop me."

In the last ten years, Dr. Kevorkian has helped over 130 people die. All these people, he points out, wanted to die. Some had terminal diseases. Others were in unbearable pain. His first patient was Janet Adkins, age 54, who had Alzheimer's disease. She and her family went to Dr. Kevorkian because they knew that she would get much worse. She wanted to avoid the future pain and suffering. He talked for a long time with her and her family, and when they convinced him of their wishes, he agreed to help. He put together a device that injected her when she turned on the switches. Within seconds she was dead. A peaceful look was on her face. She died with her family around her.

Dr. Kevorkian has been on trial in the state of Michigan several times. All of the earlier cases were either thrown out or he was found not guilty of assisted suicide. However, he seemed to go a bit further with his last patient, a man suffering from a serious muscular disease. Dr. Kevorkian himself injected him with the deadly chemicals. The patient and his family supported Dr. Kevorkian, but the state charged him with assisted suicide and brought him to trial. Dr. Kevorkian was found guilty.

If euthanasia becomes legal, some people worry that it might change our attitudes toward the sick and old in our society. They worry that it will become a solution to the expensive medical care that the sick and old need. Instead of taking care of the sick and elderly, we will just get rid of them. Euthanasia also contradicts the Hippocratic oath, which all doctors swear to follow. This oath, dating from ancient Greece, upholds the value of human life. A physician promises to protect

(continued)

life, not to end it. Another fear is that governments change and their attitudes toward their citizens change. Euthanasia brings memories of Nazi Germany, where people were killed because they were different. On the other hand, we put to sleep a household pet that is old or sick. When a horse breaks a leg, they shoot the horse. Do we treat animals better than we treat humans?

There isn't a satisfactory answer to this difficult question. Dr. Kevorkian argues, "My . . . voice cannot accomplish much. But . . . in taking action through . . . medicine as the first step in the right direction, I have done all I can on behalf of a just cause. . ." Dr. Kevorkian is a sincere man who has a following. His cause will continue.

B. Draw a line through the incorrect answers. Some have more than one answer.

1. Dr. Kevorkian is (Dr. Death / a pathologist / retired / terminally ill).

2. His first patient was (a woman / an Alzheimer's patient / a man / 54 years old).

3. Dr. Kevorkian (is a simple man / lives in a luxurious home / is a musician / has a lot of clothes).

4. He believes that assisted suicide is (a just cause / a medical issue / a legal issue / done for a greater good).

5. The Hippocratic oath (respects life / supports assisted suicide / is a doctor's code of ethics / is over 2,000 years old).

6. Euthanasia is legal (for animals / everywhere / in Michigan / for doctors.)

C. Answer these questions. Discuss your answers with a partner.

1. What kind of person is Dr. Kevorkian?

2. How many people has he helped?

3. How does Dr. Kevorkian feel about the laws against assisted suicide?

4. What are the points in favor of assisted suicide?

5. What are the points against assisted suicide?

6. How do you feel about Dr. Kevorkian? How do you feel about his cause?

Opinion Survey: Life Support

A. Complete the survey. Circle *A* if you agree or *D* if you disagree. If you are not sure, circle *?*.

1. Doctors should use life-support machines for all patients near death.	A	D	?
2. Doctors should help a seriously ill patient to die if the patient requests it.	A	D	?
3. Doctors should use life-support machines only for patients who can afford to pay.	A	D	?
4. Doctors should use life-support machines only for young patients.	A	D	?
5. Doctors should not use life-support machines for patients with terminal diseases.	A	D	?
6. Euthanasia should be legal.	A	D	?
7. Only doctors should help a sick person die.	A	D	?
8. People should die at home.	A	D	?
9. Dying is like birth, and people should help in both events.	A	D	?
10. Assisted suicide is wrong because of the possibility of a cure.	A	D	?

B. Compare your answers with a partner. Use verbs such as *think* and *believe* to report your partner's answers to the class.

Example

Alison thinks that doctors should use life-support systems for all patients near death.

Pronunciation	Contractions with *should*

When *should* is contracted with *not,* it often sounds like *shu-un.*

1 Listen to your teacher read this dialogue.

REPORTER: What should doctors do about terminally ill patients?

NURSE: It depends. Every case is different.

REPORTER: We shouldn't put every patient on life support, should we?

NURSE: I don't think so. We shouldn't because it's very expensive.

REPORTER: Should a doctor help a patient die if he or she requests it?

NURSE: Certainly not. A doctor shouldn't help a patient commit suicide. It's against the law.

2 Repeat the dialogue after your teacher.

3 With a partner, practice the dialogue between the reporter and the nurse.

Written Reaction

A. Match the words and phrases with their meanings.

___f___ 1. vegetative state

_____ 2. guarded but stable condition

_____ 3. nutrients

_____ 4. pros and cons

_____ 5. terminal disease/illness

_____ 6. controversial

_____ 7. thin and frail

_____ 8. unbearable pain

_____ 9. agonizing

a. suffering and discomfort that is too much for a sick person

b. food

c. causing worry or great pain

d. sickness that will kill the person who has it

e. underweight and weak

f. a condition when a sick person shows no reactions or senses for a long time

g. a condition when a seriously sick person doesn't get better and doesn't get worse

h. causing a lot of positive or negative public reaction

i. advantages and disadvantages

B. Write five sentences about things that Mrs. Hernandez and her daughter can't do.

Example

They can't breathe without life-support machines.

1. _____

2. _____

3. _____

4. _____

5. _____

C. Read the reports on page 97 again. Write the next two reports about the conditions of Mrs. Hernandez and her daughter, Juanita.

D. What are your feelings about life support or euthanasia? Do you agree or disagree with Dr. Kevorkian? Write a paragraph for the newspaper stating your feelings. Create your own title.

Unit Sixteen

After-School Job

Reaction

How do you feel about a part-time job for a high school student?
What are some possible problems when high school students work?

Interaction

A. Read about the situation.

Larry Goforth is a sixteen-year-old high school student who loves cars, particularly 1966 Mustangs. He wants to buy one and fix it up. His parents don't have the money, so he decided to get a job after school. In the newspaper he saw an ad for a stock boy at a car-parts store. He went to the interview and got the job. It's his first job—three hours a day after school and all day on Saturday. He loves it. He's around cars. He's learning from watching others and now has money of his own. He dreams of getting that Mustang, but school has taken a back seat. His parents are worried.

Read the conversations Larry has at school, at work and at home.

1. MRS. PIERCE: Larry, did you study for this test?

   LARRY: Not much, Mrs. Pierce.

   MRS. PIERCE: How do you expect to pass if you don't study?

   LARRY: I didn't have much time. I had to work last night.

   MRS. PIERCE: You're a bright boy, Larry, but I'm beginning to get concerned about your chances of passing this class.

Larry at School

2. MR. HARVEY: Larry, when you finish that job, start unpacking the boxes that just arrived.

   LARRY: Yes, sir. No problem.

   MR. HARVEY: You know, Larry, you have a good future in this business. You stick with me and I'll show you the ropes.

   LARRY: That's what I want, Mr. Harvey, but my parents want me to finish school.

   MR. HARVEY: Well, school is important, but . . .

Larry at Work

3. MRS. GOFORTH: Larry, how are you doing in school? Mrs. Pierce called me.

   LARRY: Ma, I'm not interested in school. I have a job now.

   MR. GOFORTH: But, son, we want you to finish school and go to college.

   LARRY: Well, Mr. Harvey says I have a bright future in the car-parts business and I can learn the ropes from him.

   MRS. GOFORTH: Do you want to work as a stock boy the rest of your life?

Larry at Home

B. Circle *T* if the statement is true or *F* if the statement is false. If you don't know, circle *?*.

1. Larry's parents are pleased that he has an after-school job.	T	F	?
2. Larry is a good math student.	T	F	?
3. Larry's boss thinks he should finish school.	T	F	?
4. Larry's teacher knows about his after-school job.	T	F	?
5. Larry wants to buy his own car.	T	F	?
6. Larry wants to be a stock boy the rest of his life.	T	F	?
7. Larry wants to finish school.	T	F	?
8. Larry's parents agree with him about his future.	T	F	?

C. Answer these questions. Compare your answers with a partner.

1. What is Larry like at home? At school? At work?
2. What do Larry's parents want him to do?
3. What does Mrs. Pierce want him to do?
4. What does Mr. Harvey want him to do?
5. What does Larry want to do?
6. What do you think Mr. Harvey's advice is about finishing school?

D. Discuss these questions in a small group.

1. At what age is it O.K. for a young person to work?
2. For some jobs, you don't need much education. What are some of these jobs?
3. Why is education important in life?
4. What do/did your parents want for you?
5. If you have children, what do you want for them?
6. What do you want for yourself?
7. How can a part-time job help a young person?
8. How can it hurt a young person?

Reading Reaction

A. Before reading the article, think about these questions.

- What was your first job like?
- Why do some young people work?

My First Job

by Heather Baldwin

When I was fifteen, I had a part-time job. I was a newspaper boy—well, a newspaper girl. My parents weren't enthusiastic about it, but I delivered the daily newspaper, the *Charlotte Observer*, every morning. I had to get up very early—around 5 A.M.—because people wanted to read their newspapers while they were having breakfast. A newspaper and a morning cup of coffee seem to go together.

At first I delivered the newspapers on my bicycle, but the newspapers were heavy and the route was long. By the time I finished, I was really tired. Then I had to go to school. So my dad offered to let me drive the old Ford truck. I folded the newspapers and placed them in a pile on the seat beside me. At each house on the route, I grabbed a folded newspaper from the seat and threw it on each doorstep. Many times, the customers were waiting for the newspaper and waved as I drove by. Often they were able to catch the newspaper.

Sometimes a neighborhood dog would run by and try to catch the newspapers when I threw them. When that happened, I stopped the truck, caught the dog, removed the slightly soggy newspaper from his mouth, and took it to the door. Mrs. Wiley's dog, Jethro, was the worst. Then, I learned that she kept him in the house during the night and let him out in the morning. I found out the time she let Jethro out and planned my deliveries before Jethro's exit. Those dog incidents always delayed me.

One morning at the Thompson house, I threw the newspaper so hard that it hit the door window. The Thompson house was one of the oldest and finest houses in the town. The window broke—a stained glass window. Mrs. Thompson called my mother, and I had to pay for the repair of the glass. Wow, that was expensive.

At that time I hated that job, but I wanted to buy a motorbike. When I had the money, I quit delivering newspapers. To this day, however, I remember certain things about that job. Mrs. Thompson's kindness comes to my memory. (She allowed me to pay for the window in installments). I remember the bond that developed between Jethro and me. I also remember the beauty of those spring mornings, when a moment was not just a moment but a glimpse of eternity. The morning fog, the mists from the fields, and the bright rising sun with its many colors blessed the world that I knew at that time.

B. Circle *T* if the statement is true, *F* if the statement is false. If you don't know, circle *?*.

1. The writer liked her first job. T F ?
2. Her parents were enthusiastic about her job. T F ?
3. She wanted to make money to repair a window. T F ?
4. She became acquainted with many of her customers. T F ?
5. The writer lived in a small town. T F ?
6. She worked at this job for a long time. T F ?
7. She bought a bicycle with her money. T F ?
8. The writer had good memories of her first job. T F ?

C. Answer these questions. Discuss your answers with a partner.

1. What sort of job did the writer of this article have?
2. What change did she make after doing the job for a little while?
3. What were some of the difficulties of this job?
4. What were some of the good memories of this job?
5. Who was Mrs. Thompson? Mrs. Wiley? Jethro?
6. What are some memories of your first job?

Opinion Survey: Education and Teenagers

A. Complete the survey. Circle *A* if you agree or *D* if you disagree with these statements. If you don't know, circle *?*.

1. It's a good idea for students to have part-time jobs that teach them responsibility. A D ?
2. You don't have to attend school to be educated. A D ?
3. If a person can make a living, education isn't so important. A D ?
4. Formal education, in general, prepares people to make a living. A D ?
5. Parents should let their children decide about their own education. A D ?
6. Education is more important than money. A D ?
7. Teenagers today have too much money. A D ?
8. Teenagers should volunteer in the community. A D ?
9. Teenagers should help around the house rather than have a part-time job. A D ?
10. Students who have part-time jobs do not do well in school. A D ?

B. Compare your answers with the other students in your class. Find out how many agree with the statements. Place this information on the following chart. Use percentages (%). Compare your charts.

Example

Forty percent of our class agreed that you don't have to attend school to be educated.

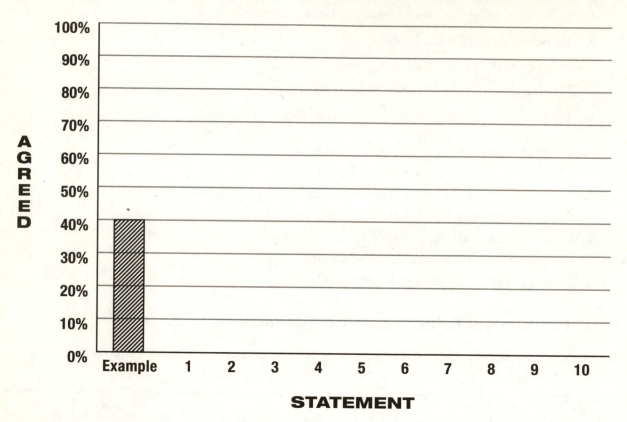

Pronunciation *Did you* and *want you*

In rapid speech *did you* often sounds like *dija*; *want you* often sounds like *wan-cha*.

1 Listen to your teacher read the dialogue.

NATALIA: What kind of job did you have when you first started working?

TAKAO: I was a guide at Disneyland.

NATALIA: Really? Did your parents want you to do that?

TAKAO: Actually, they wanted me to work in an office. How about you? Where did you first work?

NATALIA: In my father's restaurant. I was a waitress.

TAKAO: Did you want to work there?

NATALIA: It was okay. I earned enough to go to school that way.

2 Repeat the dialogue after your teacher.

3 With a partner, practice the dialogue between Natalia and Takao.

Written Reaction

A. Match the words and phrases with their meanings.

   h   1. (to) stick with someone   a. (to) stop going to school before graduating

        2. (to) show someone the ropes   b. (to) receive money for work

        3. (to) bless   c. (to) postpone

        4. (to) volunteer   d. a sense of union, unity between two people or animals

        5. (to) delay   e. (to) work without receiving money

        6. bond   f. (to) show someone how to do something

        7. (to) drop out   g. (to) wish someone good luck; to give approval

        8. (to) earn   h. (to) stay with someone

B. Write six sentences about what Larry should do. Use expressions such as *It's O.K. for . . .* , *It's a good idea for . . .* , *It's important for . . .* , or *He should . . .*

Example

It's a good idea for Larry to finish school.

1. _____

2. _____

3. _____

4. _____

5. _____

6. _____

C. Imagine that you are Larry's guidance counselor at school. Write a summary of Larry's situation, including the feelings of his parents and Mr. Harvey, and your advice to Larry.

D. Write a short description of your first job.

Unit Seventeen

Higher Education

Reaction

What sorts of privileges and problems do university students have?
What is the government's responsibility in providing higher education?

Interaction

A. Read about the situation.

Lars, Rodrigo, and Martine were good friends throughout high school. They often went out and studied together. They all have good grades, and their teachers think they are good students. All three plan to study medicine when they get to the university. Look at their university options in countries A and B.

COUNTRY A

Students take a national examination to enter any university. They will have to score in the top 10 percent of all students in the country to get into medical school at a university. Medical schools are the most difficult to enter. With a lower score, students can study another subject that is easier. Students have to spend years preparing for the university admission examination. Most of them take additional classes that prepare them for this examination. They pay a lot of money to attend special "cram schools," which are special schools to help students pass the university entrance examination. Their families also pay special teachers to help their children pass the examination. In many countries, it's shameful to fail this examination, and a few young people even commit suicide if they fail. However, if they get into the university, they pay little or nothing for their education. They don't have to study very hard, and they are usually well off the rest of their lives.

COUNTRY B

Students choose government-supported or private universities. Both government-supported and private schools charge tuition. The private schools charge a lot of tuition, while the state-supported schools charge much less. In general, the private schools are among the best, but some state-supported schools have good reputations. Some private schools, however, despite their high tuitions, are nothing more than diploma mills, which take the students' money without teaching them very much. Even the state schools vary in educational quality. State-supported schools are committed to educating the masses more than private schools. As a result, their standards are not as high. To get into most schools, it is necessary to take certain tests of verbal and mathematical ability. A private testing company develops these tests. More students have an opportunity to get a college education in this situation, but the students have to choose carefully if they want a good college education.

B. Answer these questions. Discuss your answers with a partner.

1. In which system would you prefer to study, that of Country A or Country B?
2. What are the advantages and disadvantages of Country A's system of higher education?
3. What are the advantages and disadvantages of Country B's system of higher education?
4. Are all systems of higher education like Country A's or B's?
5. What sort of pressure are students under before entering the university?
6. Who should prepare students for the entrance test for universities?
7. What are some of the ways universities select students?
8. How do you think universities should select students?

C. Read about what happened to Rodrigo. Then answer the questions with a partner.

Rodrigo wanted to study medicine in Country A, but his scores were not high enough. He changed to another specialization, but he is not really interested in this second area of study. However, it is the only way for him to get a university degree.

1. How do you think Rodrigo feels?
2. How do you think the other students in his new specialization feel?
3. Is this practice good for the university?
4. Is this practice good for society in general?
5. Rodrigo knew a student who got into medical school with the same scores he had a year earlier. What sort of circumstances might cause that to happen?

Opinion Survey: Higher Education

A. Complete the survey. Circle A if you agree or D if you disagree with these statements.

1. It's O.K. for women and men to study together in the university.	A	D
2. Universities should accept only students with the best grades.	A	D
3. Poor students need extra money from the government.	A	D
4. Students with learning disabilities should receive special services.	A	D
5. Universities must offer opportunities to everyone who wants an education.	A	D
6. If students do not pass their subjects, they should leave school.	A	D
7. The friendships and connections from the university years continue through life.	A	D
8. Grades do not matter if you have a university degree.	A	D
9. The goal of a university education is to make more money in your career.	A	D
10. University education should be free in all countries.	A	D

B. Compare your answers with the other students in your class. Find out how many agree or disagree with the statements. Use fractions to report your class's opinions.

Example

Two-thirds of the class agree that university education should be free.

Reading Reaction

A. Before reading the following letter, think about these questions.

- How do parents feel when their children go away to school?
- What are some new and different things that university students do?

November 23

Dear Mama,

Well, my university classes began, and I have much to tell you. First, my dormitory burned down. They said the fire started in my room. I fell asleep while smoking. You always told me that smoking was bad, but I didn't really believe you. Now I do.

Oh yes. I got married. His name is Todd. He's a little younger than I am—only 17—but mature for his age. He works at a gas station near the university. He likes smelling the gas. He's not interested in finishing high school. He says the teachers don't understand his learning disability.

We are living together in his small one-room apartment. The air is not so fresh because Todd smokes two packs of cigarettes a day, and there's only one small window. We don't eat very much. You know I'm not a good cook anyway. Besides, we don't have much money for food, but I have found a way to get help. I go to the post office and stand by the front door with my hand out. I ask people if they have any extra change. People are so generous. After a few months, when my stomach gets bigger, I'm sure people will be even more generous.

Yes, you guessed it: I'm pregnant. My doctor told me yesterday. The baby is due at the end of next semester. If I'm lucky, I can finish the semester before the baby comes. Then I'll have to stop classes to take care of the baby. If it's a little girl, we'll name her after you. Maybe a baby will stop Todd from drinking so much. When he drinks, he gets violent, but it's O.K. if I stay out of his way. Sometimes, just to make him feel better, I take a drink with him. It also helps me sleep.

(continued)

Well, that's my news from the university. Oh, by the way, Mom, not a word of this is true. There is no Todd. I'm not married. I'm not pregnant. The dormitory didn't burn down. I wasn't smoking in bed. In fact, I don't smoke anymore. I don't drink. I don't ask for money at the post office, but there is something you should know: I'm failing chemistry. I just wanted you to know that there are worse things than failing chemistry. I love you. Oh, one more thing: Can you send me some money so I don't have to go to the post office?

Your loving daughter,

Effie

B. Circle *T* if the statement is true or *F* if the statement is false.

1. Todd is a high-school dropout.   T   F
2. Effie stopped smoking.   T   F
3. Effie needs money.   T   F
4. Effie has a problem with one of her courses.   T   F
5. Todd is a new university student.   T   F
6. Effie is married.   T   F
7. Effie asks for money at the post office.   T   F
8. Effie tells the truth in the beginning of her letter.   T   F

C. Circle the correct answer(s). Some statements have more than one answer.

1. Effie is (pregnant / married / failing chemistry / a smoker).

2. Effie says that she (drinks / eats a lot / works at the post office / is passing all her classes).

3. She says that Todd is (a student / a smoker / her husband / living in the dormitory).

4. She says that Todd's apartment doesn't have (much light / many windows / a kitchen / clean air).

5. She says that (she is pregnant / the baby is a girl / the baby will have her mother's name / the baby is due this semester).

6. Effie says that Todd (smokes / asks for money at the post office / drinks / is a good cook).

7. Effie's real reason(s) for writing this letter is / are to (describe her university experience / make her mother feel thankful / talk about her new friends / prepare her mother for bad news / ask for money).

8. Todd (works at a gas station / doesn't exist / is another student / is Effie's boyfriend).

D. Answer these questions. Discuss your answers with a partner.

1. What does Effie say about Todd?
2. What does Effie say about herself?
3. How does she describe her living conditions?
4. How does she say she makes extra money?
5. What are some of the surprises she tells her mother?
6. What does Effie say that is *not* true?
7. What is Effie's real purpose in writing this letter to her mother?
8. If you were Effie's mother, how would you feel?

Pronunciation   Intonation in *if* clauses

When a sentence begins with an *if* clause, there is a slight pause after the *if* clause, which is shown by a comma in writing, and the voice rises at the end of the *if* clause. When the *if* clause ends the sentence, the voice falls at the end of the sentence.

1 Listen to your teacher read these sentences.
   a. If students want a good college education, they must choose carefully.
   b. Some young people commit suicide if they fail.
   c. If Mary gets into the university, she won't pay tuition.
   d. Older adults should have the opportunity to study if they wish.
   e. If students don't pass their courses, they should leave school.
   f. Grades don't matter if you have a university degree.
   g. If it's a little girl, we'll name her after you.
   h. If I'm lucky, I'll finish the semester.

2 Repeat the sentences after your teacher.
3 With a partner, practice saying the sentences.

Written Reaction

A. Match the phrases with their meanings.

___f___ 1. learning disability
_____ 2. (to) fail
_____ 3. shameful
_____ 4. (to) be well off
_____ 5. (to) charge tuition
_____ 6. (to) have a good reputation
_____ 7. (to) vary in quality
_____ 8. the masses

a. (to) receive an unsatisfactory grade in a class
b. the majority of people
c. (to) have differing standards of excellence
d. (to) be well respected by other people
e. (to) require students to pay for their education
f. problem that causes a person difficulty in reading and writing
g. (to) be rich
h. disgraceful, dishonorable

B. Write three advantages and three disadvantages of studying in a government-supported university.

Advantages

1. _____

2. _____

3. _____

Disadvantages

1. _____

2. _____

3. _____

C. Write three advantages and three disadvantages of studying in a private university.

Advantages

1. _____

2. _____

3. _____

Disadvantages

1. _____

2. _____

3. _____

D. Write a paragraph explaining your feelings about university education. Create your own title.

Unit Eighteen

Peer Pressure

Reaction

What do these young people like to do?

What problems do young people have today?

Interaction

Read the chart and circle your answers.
F = *only girls;* M = *only boys;* B = *both boys and girls;* N = *neither girls nor boys*

	Things They Do	Is Peer Pressure Involved?		Do Most Parents Approve?		Who Is This Important To?			
1.	Wear stylish clothes	Yes	No	Yes	No	F	M	B	N
2.	Hang out in popular places	Yes	No	Yes	No	F	M	B	N
3.	Read books	Yes	No	Yes	No	F	M	B	N
4.	Use the telephone	Yes	No	Yes	No	F	M	B	N
5.	Watch popular TV shows and movies	Yes	No	Yes	No	F	M	B	N
6.	Visit older relatives	Yes	No	Yes	No	F	M	B	N
7.	Play sports	Yes	No	Yes	No	F	M	B	N
8.	Listen to popular music	Yes	No	Yes	No	F	M	B	N
9.	Attend religious services regularly	Yes	No	Yes	No	F	M	B	N
10.	Use the Internet	Yes	No	Yes	No	F	M	B	N
11.	Have the latest hairstyle	Yes	No	Yes	No	F	M	B	N
12.	Study	Yes	No	Yes	No	F	M	B	N
13.	Other	Yes	No	Yes	No	F	M	B	N

Things Young People Do

A. In small groups, discuss these questions.

1. How do most people (adults or young people) respond to peer pressure?
2. When is peer pressure good? When is it bad?
3. How do you react to peer pressure?
4. How do young people feel when adults do things they tell young people not to do?
5. If you are an adult, which things did you do because of peer pressure that you now regret?
6. Which things have you not done because of your parents' disapproval?
7. Is parent approval or disapproval more important than peer pressure? Why or why not?

Reading Reaction

A. Before reading the selection, think about these questions.

- Why is it so important for young people to feel that they belong?
- What sorts of things do young people do to get attention or to identify themselves with a particular group?

Wake Up America!

by Pat Riotique

Most everybody wants to belong—to be a part of a group. Young people in their teens are particularly sensitive. Conformity is very important to them. They dress alike, talk alike, belong to the same clubs, and hang out together. Yet, not everyone is popular. Not everyone is a star athlete. Not everyone gets the best grades. Not everyone is the president of the student body or a popular club member. In other words, somebody has to follow. Yet there are many ways for young people to participate. Many start their own clubs and social groups. One such group was the "trench coat mafia," a group of students at Columbine High School in Littleton, Colorado, a small, prosperous city.

We don't know very much about the members of the trench coat mafia, but they were not very popular. Other students described them as "outsiders" and "strange." They all dressed in black raincoats, called trench coats. They were fascinated with World War II and the Nazis. They didn't fit in with other students, but no one realized just how dangerous these students were. On Tuesday, April 20, 1999, two of them did a horrible thing. Dressed in their black trench coats, they walked into Columbine High School and started shooting. (Coincidentally, April 20 was Adolf Hitler's birthday.)

They were heavily armed. They started their attack in the cafeteria and then moved to the library, where most of the killings occurred. They wanted revenge. The purpose was to kill popular students—those students who were star athletes, who made high grades, or who were club leaders. When it was over, there were twenty-five injured people, fourteen dead students, and one dead teacher. The two killers had also shot themselves. Furthermore, they left bombs and booby traps throughout the school building— enough to destroy it entirely. The police searched very slowly and carefully. As a result, the school was closed for the rest of the

(continued)

school year. It was a shocking, senseless tragedy. What could possibly cause two young men to do such a thing? Was it peer pressure from within their own group? Were they poor students? Did they have problems at home?

Certainly the members of the trench coat mafia spent a lot of time together. They were not the usual outsiders. Their families were well off. They even had their own cars. They were intelligent—computer whizzes who had their own web pages. From the computer, they learned to make explosives, like pipe bombs. Through an older friend, they were able to buy weapons and ammunition, which they used that terrible day.

Peer pressure may push many young people to commit illegal activities that may cause others or themselves harm. The Colorado tragedy is just one of the signs of this problem. Why are young kids giving in to the bad influence of peer pressure? Wake up America! We have a crisis on our hands!

B. Circle *T* if the statement is true or *F* if the statement is false. If you don't know, circle *?*.

1. The members of the trench coat mafia were popular.   T   F   ?

2. They didn't belong to a club.   T   F   ?

3. They had a history of violent acts against other students.   T   F   ?

4. They attempted to kill all the teachers in the school.   T   F   ?

5. All their victims were students.   T   F   ?

6. They learned about guns on the computer.   T   F   ?

7. There were only two members of the trench coat mafia.   T   F   ?

8. These kids probably felt better about themselves when they dressed alike.   T   F   ?

C. Answer these questions. Discuss your answers with a partner.

1. What was the trench coat mafia?

2. What sort of families did the killers come from?

3. How were they different from other students?

4. Who did the two young men want to kill? Why?

5. How many people were actually injured or killed?

6. What would you recommend to a parent whose child decides to join a similar group or organization?

Opinion Survey: Gun Control

A. Complete the survey. Circle *A* if you agree or *D* if you disagree with the statements.

1. Adults should teach children how to use guns.	A	D
2. The Internet should not have information about guns and explosives.	A	D
3. Only the police should have guns.	A	D
4. It's O.K. to have a gun for hunting.	A	D
5. It's O.K. to collect guns as a hobby.	A	D
6. A person who owns guns has a psychological problem.	A	D
7. The police should investigate everyone who wants to buy a gun.	A	D
8. Guns don't kill people; people with guns kill people.	A	D
9. Women who live alone should have a gun.	A	D
10. A person who was in prison should not have a gun.	A	D

B. Compare your answers with a partner. Discuss four statements in more detail.

Example

I think that adults shouldn't teach children about guns, but my partner doesn't agree.

Pronunciation — Past Tense *-ed*

The regular past tense ending *-ed* sounds like *id* as in *shouted*, *t* as in *walked*, or *d* as in *occurred*.

id	*t*	*d*
If the base verb ends in -t and -d	If the base verb ends in -k, -p, -s, -sh, -ch, or the -f sound	If the base verb ends in any other sound

1 Listen to your teacher read the past tense of these verbs. Write them in the correct column.

occur	protect	walk	shout	describe	attempt
dress	realize	dance	influence	settle	listen
want	chat	search	establish	learn	drop
start	injure	kill	belong	compensate	collect
collect	wash	use	play	type	watch

id	*t*	*d*
shouted	walked	occurred
_____	_____	_____
_____	_____	_____
_____	_____	_____

2 Repeat the verbs after your teacher.

3 With a partner, practice saying the verbs.

Written Reaction

A. Match the words and phrases with their meanings.

___f___ 1. conformity   a. (to) stay at a place for a long period of time without doing anything

_____ 2. (to) hang out   b. (to) belong

_____ 3. (to) participate   c. (to) show strength in one area because of a weakness in another

_____ 4. (to) fit in   d. bullets

_____ 5. (to) compensate for   e. (to) be active (in a club or other group)

_____ 6. innocent bystander   f. being like other people in a group

_____ 7. ammunition   g. gun, rifle, pistol, etc.

_____ 8. weapon   h. an onlooker who is not involved in a crime

B. Write five things that young people do today.

Example

Many young people get tattoos.

1. _____
2. _____
3. _____
4. _____
5. _____

C. Write five things that parents do but do not want their children to do.

Example

Parents stay up late at night.

1. _____
2. _____
3. _____
4. _____
5. _____

D. Write your opinion about peer pressure and how it plays a role in young people's lives. Create your own title.

E. Write your opinion of gun control. Talk about young people, violence, and other factors. Create your own title.

Unit Nineteen

The Breadwinner

Reaction

What are the wife's responsibilities in a marriage? The husband's?
How are the roles of husbands and wives changing today?

Interaction

A. Margaret and Douglas plan to get married and have a family. However, they have problems concerning their responsibilities in the marriage. Read about each of them.

Margaret

Margaret started as a secretary to Ms. Khan, an editor in a publishing company. She finished her college degree at night. She worked hard and advanced in the company. Now she is an executive editor. It's a wonderful job with a good salary. She feels that she has a good career in publishing and does not want to give up her job. She wants to get married now. She sees no reason to wait. She thinks that she makes enough money for an entire family—if Douglas will just swallow his pride. She does not mind being the breadwinner if Douglas will agree to take care of the house and their children.

Douglas

Douglas has a degree in architecture but cannot find a job. In order to make a living, he is working as a carpenter. He isn't making much money. Recently he received a job offer from a company in the Middle East as a highly paid architect. However, the company will pay only for him to live there. He can't bring any family members with him. He wants to postpone the marriage until he returns from the Middle East. By then, he will have more money as a nest egg for his marriage. As a proud man, he does not feel good about Margaret being the breadwinner.

B. Circle *T* if the statement is true or *F* if the statement is false. If you do not know, circle *?*.

1. Margaret and Douglas are married.	T	F	?
2. Both Margaret and Douglas have good jobs.	T	F	?
3. Douglas has a job offer and a good future with the company.	T	F	?
4. Margaret has a better education than Douglas.	T	F	?
5. Both Douglas and Margaret want to get married now.	T	F	?
6. Margaret can't swallow her pride.	T	F	?
7. Douglas doesn't mind taking care of the house and children.	T	F	?
8. Margaret and Douglas love each other.	T	F	?

C. Answer these questions. Discuss your answers with a partner.

1. How does Margaret feel about being the breadwinner? What are Douglas's feelings? Why do they feel this way?

2. How would this situation change if Douglas had the better job? How would the situation change if Margaret had the opportunity to work abroad?

3. What sorts of adjustments will Margaret and Douglas need to make if Margaret wants to continue her career?

4. Is it a good idea for Margaret and Douglas to have children?

5. Margaret and Douglas have several options for their situation, including going their separate ways. What are some other options?

6. Some international companies want their employees to take their families with them when working abroad. Others, as in Douglas's case, ask their employees to go alone. What are the reasons for each of these policies?

7. Discuss other situations when it is necessary for a happily married couple to live apart. How do you feel about living apart from your loved one(s)?

D. Role Play: Work with a partner. Imagine that you are Margaret or Douglas. Student A: Read the information about Margaret. Student B: Read the information about Douglas. Find a solution to the problem in the reading on page 124. Ask questions like "What do you want to do?" or "What do you think we should do?" and use phrases such as "I think" and "Well, I'd like to."

Margaret wants to:	**Margaret doesn't want to:**
be the breadwinner	be dependant
continue her career in publishing	stop her career
stay in this country	leave the country
get married right away	wait for marriage
have a child immediately after marriage	remain childless

Douglas wants to:	**Douglas doesn't want to:**
be the breadwinner	depend on his wife
have his own career as an architect	miss this job opportunity
take a job overseas	get married right away
postpone the marriage	have children right away
wait a few years before having children	stay in his present job

Reading Reaction

A. Before reading the selection, think about these questions.

- How has the typical American family changed over the past 25 years?
- Who earns the money to support the family?

THE BREADWINNER IN THE TYPICAL AMERICAN FAMILY

Just what is the typical American family? Father, mother, and two or three children? Guess again. According to the latest census, less than 50 percent of American households have both a father and mother present. Over 50 percent are single-parent households. They are single parents because of divorce or because the parents decided not to marry at all. Of those homes with both a mother and father under the same roof, only a select few are made up of a couple in their first marriage and with their own biological children. In most of those families, one (or both) of the parents has probably been married before and has children from the previous marriage. This creates the stepfamily: stepmother, stepfather, stepbrother, and so forth. Sometimes a couple who has children from previous marriages decide to have children together—creating half-siblings. It can be pretty complicated explaining how all the members of your family are related!

So who is the breadwinner in these families? Well, since the majority of American homes are headed by one parent, the answer is clear. The parent who has custody of the children earns the money to support the family. In most of those cases it's the mother. For the rest of the households where there is a mother and father in the same home, chances are they both work. The high cost of living in most parts of the United States doesn't allow most women to stay home to take care of the family. In some cases it's not a necessity for the woman to work. Many times when a couple decides to have kids, the mother continues to work part-time so that she can keep her career going. That way, when she wants to work full-time, she can go back to her career much more easily. If she waits too long to work again after having children, it will be like starting all over.

(continued)

Well, if the financial situation is tough for a two-income family, what about the majority of households with just one income? What about those single-parent households? You guessed it—it's even tougher for them. There may be some financial support from the other parent or from the government, but the main part of the family income is from that one parent. To save money, they might live with extended family or share a home with another single parent with children. In the end, it's up to the one person to pay the bills and put food on the table.

Times are changing, and whether it is good or bad, the facts are there: The typical American family is not the one we had twenty-five to thirty years ago. All aspects of our society, including the government, financial institutions, and employers, need to adapt to the changing situation.

B. Circle *T* if the statement is true or *F* if the statement is false.

1. The majority of American households are headed by one parent.   T   F

2. Most American families with a father and a mother under the same roof are headed by a couple in their first marriage.   T   F

3. Having a stepbrother or half-sister is uncommon in the United States.   T   F

4. The father usually has custody of children in a single-parent situation.   T   F

5. Nowadays, most mothers work at some point during their children's lives.   T   F

6. Sometimes single parents live together with their families to save money.   T   F

C. Answer these questions. Discuss your answers with a partner.

1. How many American households have both a father and mother present?
2. Why are there so many single-parent households?
3. What are half-siblings?
4. How does a single parent receive money to support the household?
5. Why do many American mothers work?
6. Why are there so few households where the mother is able to stay home to take care of the family?

Opinion Survey: Marriage Responsibilities

A. Complete the survey. Circle *W* if you think the responsibility is the wife's, *H* if you think it is the husband's, *E* if you think it is either person's responsibility, or *B* if you think it is both people's responsibility.

		W	H	E	B
1. Takes care of the children.		W	H	E	B
2. Cleans the house.		W	H	E	B
3. Cooks the meals.		W	H	E	B
4. Manages the family budget/finances.		W	H	E	B
5. Has a career.		W	H	E	B
6. Shops for food.		W	H	E	B
7. Takes care of the family car.		W	H	E	B
8. Decorates the home.		W	H	E	B
9. Chooses the TV programs/movies.		W	H	E	B
10. Talks to the children's teachers.		W	H	E	B

B. Compare your answers with a partner. Then, in a group, report your answer to each item. Use *and* or *but* to compare your answers to your partner's.

Examples

I think it's the responsibility of the wife to take care of the children, and Tomoko thinks so, too.

I think it's the responsibility of the wife to take care of the children, but Ahmed doesn't think so.

Pronunciation   Possessive *'s*

The *'s* ending of possessive nouns has three different sounds: *iz* as in *Douglas's, s* as in *Margaret's,* or *z* as in *Tomoko's.*

iz	*s*	*z*
Nouns ending in -s, -z, -j, -sh, -ch	Nouns ending in -t, -p, -k, -f, and -th	Nouns ending in all other sounds

1 Listen to your teacher read this dialogue.

2 Repeat the dialogue after your teacher.

IRENE: Douglas's new job is a great opportunity for him.

MANNY: But the two of them can live on Margaret's salary.

IRENE: Douglas's pride won't allow him to do that. Besides, he doesn't think Margaret's position is that good. It's only an editor's position.

MANNY: Well, Douglas's present job isn't that good either. Mr. Tomayo's company is in financial trouble, I hear.

IRENE: Too bad. It seems to be a problem between Douglas's opportunity and Margaret's career. I suppose their marriage will have to wait for a while.

3 With a partner, practice the dialogue.

Written Reaction

A. Match the words and phrases with their meanings.

  _c_   1. career   a. the person who earns the money for the family

_____ 2. (to) swallow one's pride   b. money one has to spend for a specific use

_____ 3. role   c. job, profession

_____ 4. responsibility   d. money saved for the future

_____ 5. breadwinner   e. person's function

_____ 6. nest egg   f. (to) do what is best even if it hurts

_____ 7. budget   g. obligation

B. Write five sentences to explain the differences between Margaret and Douglas.

Example

Margaret has a better job.

1. _____

2. _____

3. _____

4. _____

5. _____

C. Margaret and Douglas decide to write to Cordelia, a woman with an advice column in the newspaper, for help with their problem. Write their letter. Give information about each one and state what each wants to do.

D. Write a description of the typical modern family in your country.

On My Own

Reaction

How does this picture make you feel? Why?
Where do you think she is going?

Interaction

A. **Answer these questions. Discuss your answers with a partner.**
1. What are some bad things that could happen to young people on their own?
2. What are some good things that young people learn when they are on their own?
3. What are some of the conflicts between parents and adolescents as the children become adults?
4. How do parents influence their children?
5. Why do some people think it is better for young people to live at home until they get married?

B. **Read the conversation between Mr. and Mrs. Crinshaw and their son Mark.**

MR. CRINSHAW: But you're not old enough to leave home.

MARK: Dad, I'm eighteen.

MR. CRINSHAW: When I was your age, I . . .

MARK: Times are different now. Many of my friends have their own places.

MRS. CRINSHAW: Where are you going to live?

MARK: I'm going to share an apartment. The arrangements are made.

MRS. CRINSHAW: Share an apartment? Who with?

MARK: With my friend Max.

MRS. CRINSHAW: And who's Max? What kind of person is he?

MARK: Max is a girl, Ma. Her real name's Maxine. She's my best friend.

MRS. CRINSHAW: Oh, my goodness. What will Grandma think when she hears this?

MARK: I talked with Grandma already, and she thinks it's a good idea. It's time for me to be on my own.

C. **Circle *T* if the statement is true or *F* if the statement is false. If you don't know, circle *?*.**

	T	F	?
1. Mark is going to get married.	T	F	?
2. Grandma disapproves of Mark's leaving home.	T	F	?
3. Mark is going to move to Grandma's house.	T	F	?
4. Mark is going to share an apartment.	T	F	?
5. Mark's parents know Max.	T	F	?
6. Grandma knows Max.	T	F	?
7. Mark's parents disapprove of his leaving home.	T	F	?
8. Mark's parents think he's too immature to leave home.	T	F	?

D. **Answer these questions about the conversation. Discuss your answers with a partner.**
1. What are Mark's plans?
2. How many family members know of Mark's plans?
3. How do Mark's parents feel about his moving out?
4. What two surprises does Mark tell his parents?
5. Who is Max?
6. What is Grandma's opinion?
7. Why are Mark's parents so upset?
8. How do you think Max's parents feel about the situation?

E. **Role Play: With a partner, choose one of the following situations and create a conversation.**
1. Mark and Max talk about their parents' reactions to the news.
2. Mark and Grandma talk about his moving out of his parents' home.
3. Mark and his parents talk about other options they did not discuss in the dialogue.

Reading Reaction

A. **Before reading the selection, think about these questions.**
- How do most older people feel about young people today?
- How do most younger people feel about old people today?

WHAT'S WRONG WITH YOUNG PEOPLE TODAY?
by Al Codger

What's wrong with young people today? I live in the city, and a lot of young people gather on my corner. They belong to a gang, the Blackbirds, but to me they look like wet chickens. Some of them drink and smoke. I also hear some foul language. They always have a radio on, but it's not music they listen to. It's noise—some guy rapping. What a weird-looking gathering they are—swinging and bobbing in rhythm. They dress alike, both boys and girls—black boots and black clothing. And their makeup is unbelievable—green and purple hair, dark lipstick, and nail polish. They're all into body decoration. They pierce different parts of their bodies. Not just their ears; they pierce their noses, their belly buttons, even their eyebrows. Most of them have tattoos. I know one boy who has a snake tattoo that coils all the way up his arm. He's my grandson, Seth. He's a good kid, but back in my day it was different.

B. Circle *T* if the statement is true or *F* if the statement is false. If you don't know, circle *?*.

1. This article is by a young person.   T   F   ?

2. This writer lives in the neighborhood mentioned in the article.   T   F   ?

3. The writer thinks all young people are like those in his
   neighborhood.   T   F   ?

4. The writer thinks that boys and girls dress differently.   T   F   ?

5. The writer doesn't like these young people.   T   F   ?

6. The writer criticizes the young people's appearance.   T   F   ?

7. The writer says these young people belong to a club.   T   F   ?

8. The writer doesn't know these young people.   T   F   ?

C. Based on the article, answer the following questions. Discuss your answers with a partner.

1. Who is the writer of this article?

2. How does he feel about young people in the beginning?

3. What does he say about young people?

4. What is his surprise at the end?

Pronunciation   *Going to*

In rapid speech, the future expression *going to* often sounds like *gonna*.

1 Listen to your teacher read this dialogue.

GRANDMA: Where are you going to live?

MARK: In an apartment.

GRANDMA: Are you going to pay the rent by yourself?

MARK: No, Max is going to share with me.

GRANDMA: Oh, you're going to be O.K. then.

2 Repeat the dialogue after your teacher.

3 With a partner, practice the dialogue.

Opinion Survey: Young People Today

A. Complete this survey. Write a ✔ if you think it's O.K. for a boy or girl to do these things. Write an *X* if you don't think it's O.K.

It's O.K. for young people to	Boys	Girls
1. stay out as late as they wish.		
2. smoke.		
3. wear whatever they want.		
4. drink alcohol.		
5. earn their own money.		
6. play sports.		
7. spend a lot of time alone.		
8. belong to gangs.		
9. have older friends.		
10. learn to defend themselves.		

B. Compare your answers with those of your classmates. Find out how many students think it's O.K. for boys and girls to do these things. Then, with a partner, ask each other questions about your class's opinions. In your answers use expressions such as: *none, not many, a few, several, many, most,* and *all.*

Example

STUDENT A: How does the class feel about staying out late?

STUDENT B: Most of the students feel that it's O.K. for boys to stay out late. How does the class feel about young people having older friends?

STUDENT A: Not many feel that it's O.K. for young people to have older friends.

Written Reaction

A. Complete the description of young people. Use the words or phrases from the box.

adolescence	foul language	upset	to share
immature	disapprove	criticize	club

The teen-aged years are called _____ . It's a time when young people express
                                    1.

themselves in many different ways. They may dress in strange clothing or wear a lot of

makeup. Some of them may get involved in special activities and join a neighborhood

_____ . Some get tattoos or pierce their ears, noses, or belly buttons. Their music is
   2.

also a part of their expression, and some listen to rap, hip-hop, alternative rock, or some

other popular music. Young people probably act differently so that the other teen-agers

won't _____ them. They just want to be like everyone else. Many parents
           3.

_____ of their children's behavior. For example, most parents don't approve of
       4.

smoking, using _____ , or getting involved with the wrong group of friends.
                    5.

     Sometimes if young people aren't too _____, or too young, their parents may
                                               6.

let them move away from home. To do this, they often have _____ an apartment
                                                            7.

with a friend. When they move out, parents may be _____ because their children
                                                    8.

are now adults, and they are at last on their own.

B. **Write five things that are O.K. for young people to do.**

Example

It's O.K. for young people to earn their own money.

1. _____

2. _____

3. _____

4. _____

5. _____

C. **Write five things that are not O.K. for young people to do.**

Example

It's not O.K. for young people to smoke.

1. _____

2. _____

3. _____

4. _____

5. _____

D. **Imagine that you are Mark. Write a letter to your parents. Explain your plans to move out and give reasons to convince your parents.**

E. **Imagine that you are Mark's parents. Write an entry in a journal. Discuss Mark's plans to move out and share an apartment with a female friend. How do you feel?**

Answer Key

Note: For exercises where no answers are given, answers may vary.

Unit 1: Feelings

Reading Reaction (pages 5–6)
B. 1. man   2. amused   3. embarrassed by   4. married   5. tell the barber what you want
6. the writer's wife
C. 1. He got a haircut that he didn't like.   2. He's grown up.   3. He's retired.   4. Explain exactly what you want to the person cutting your hair.

Written Reaction (page 6)
A. 1. c   3. g   5. a   7. b
2. e   4. f   6. h   8. d

Unit 2: Picture Gallery

Interaction (page 9)
A. 1. A   3. E   5. B
2. D   4. C   6. F

Reading Reaction (pages 11–12)
B. 1. T   3. F   5. T   7. F
2. F   4. F   6. T   8. F
C. 1. He wraps large things like buildings and monuments. The art lasts only a short time.
2. Bulgaria   3. the Brandenburg Gate and the Louvre   4. He studies what he plans to wrap.   5. Answers will vary.

Written Reaction (page 13)
A. 1. c   3. f   5. d   7. g
2. h   4. b   6. a   8. e

Unit 3: Love Is Blind

Interaction (page 15)
B. 1. F   3. ?   5. ?   7. F
2. F   4. F   6. ?   8. T

Reading Reaction (page 17–19)

B. 1. mother   2. dowry   3. clergy   4. a dowry   5. Middle Eastern marriages have a low rate of divorce.   6. divorce   7. A limousine   8. A Western

Written Reaction (page 19)

A. 1. become older   2. having principles   3. traditional   4. perceive   5. different idea   6. to accept   7. negative   8. not to please

Unit 4: Desert Dilemma

Interaction (page 22)

B. *Equipment*   roll of toilet paper, mess kit, sleeping bag, book of matches, dozen flares, portable radio, wool blanket, road map, first-aid kit, large utility knife, insect repellent, tent, flare gun, flashlight, camping stove, compass, beach umbrella, cell phone, can opener, sunscreen lotion

Food   eggs, powdered milk, water, coffee, fresh fruit and vegetables, canned food

Reading Reaction (pages 23–24)

B. 1. b   3. a   5. d, e, f, h   7. c
2. a   4. d, e, f, g, h   6. d, e, f   8. d, e, f, g, h

Pronunciation (page 25)

1. 4   c. 5   e. 2   g. 5   i. 4
b. 2   d. 4   f. 4   h. 4   j. 3

Written Reaction (page 26)

A. 1. e   3. g   5. f   7. a
2. c   4. b   6. h   8. d

Unit 5: The Murder of the Earl of Hereford

Interaction (page 28)

B. 1. The earl was sitting closest to the plant. The mad scientist (daughter) was on the earl's right. The fashion model (son-in-law) was on the earl's left. The weight lifter (nephew) was across from the earl.   2. The cat was in the window closest to the plant (see picture on page 27). The location of the cat tells you where the earl was sitting.   3. There are three men and one woman.   4. mad scientist (daughter), fashion model (son-in-law), weight lifter (nephew)   5. his son-in-law because the earl's wine was closest to him.
6. Answers will vary.

Reading Reaction (pages 29–30)

B. 1. F   3. ?   5. T   7. ?
2. ?   4. T   6. ?   8. ?

C. 1. 1558–1603   2. She never married or had children.   3. She loved them.
4. The English navy became the strongest in the world under her rule, and she was well respected by other world leaders, even her enemies.   5. England became a world power, English culture and language spread, and the arts in England flourished.   6. She loved and trusted her people.   7. Princess Diana

Written Reaction (page 31)

A. 1. reign   2. insignificant   3. monarch   4. flourished   5. mighty   6. mild   7. effective

Unit 6: The Jewels Are Missing!

Interaction (page 34)

B. 1. T 3. ? 5. F
2. T 4. T 6. F

C. 1. Five: Mr. Ives, Dame Dora, Baroness Lamunda, Baron Lamunda, Colonel Headstrong (Dame Dora's niece) 2. Dame Dora—lemonade; Baroness Lamunda—tea; Baron Lamunda—coffee; Colonel Headstrong—sherry 3. Dame Dora is seated closest to the safe. Colonel Headstrong is seated across from Dame Dora. Baroness Lamunda is seated to the left of Dame Dora on the sofa. Baron Lamunda is seated to the left of the Baroness on the sofa. 4. colonel 5. Baron Lamunda and Dame Dora 6. Mr. Ives 7. Mr. Ives 8–10. Answers will vary.

Reading Reaction (pages 35–37)

B. 1. d 3. b 5. c 7. f
2. e 4. h 6. a 8. g

C. 1. in a metal box 2. in the refrigerator's freezer 3. Zesta cracker box 4. jewelry, photos of her parents and children, and newspaper announcements of family deaths and marriages 5. She wanted her possessions to be divided equally among her children, and she did not want her life extended by extraordinary means if she got very sick. 6. seeds from her garden 7. The writer planted them in his or her garden. 8. Answers will vary.

Written Reaction (page 38)

A. 1. h 3. a 5. e 7. c
2. g 4. f 6. d 8. b

Unit 7: Slow Business

Reading Reaction (pages 42–43)

B. 1. F 3. T 5. T 7. T
2. T 4. F 6. F 8. T

C. 1. in developing countries 2. They are paid very little, they work in crowded factories with poor air and light, they have no benefits or job security, and they are not paid an hourly wage. 3. clothing, electronics, rugs, and other products 4. They say they are making jobs for people who need them. 5. They can refuse to buy the products and write letters to the company.

Written Reaction (page 44)

A. 1. b 3. g 5. e 7. h
2. a 4. c 6. d 8. f

Unit 8: Making a Living

Reading Reaction (pages 49–50)

B. 1. sometimes 2. developing 3. supposed to be, usually 4. different 5. tradition 6. get paid less money than

C. 1. Sexism is discrimination based on the belief that one sex is inferior. 2. Usually woman are the victims. 3. It is most common in developing countries. 4. Through interaction with family, peers, and school. 5–6. Answers will vary.

Written Reaction (page 51)

A. 1. retirement plan 2. mentally or physically disabled 3. minimum wage 4. ambitious 5. inferior 6. mistreat 7. gender roles 8. accomplishment

Unit 9: Hot Lines!

Interaction (pages 53–55)

C. 1. e, g, h   3. a, d, i   5. b
    2. c, d, f, i   4. d, i
E. Answers will vary.

Reading Reaction (pages 56–57)

B. *Incorrect Answers:*   1. anti-union   2. lunchtimes   3. corn   4. they retired on a pension
    5. unsympathetic   6. A child fell into a machine
C. 1. "Brown lung" is a disease caused by breathing in cotton fibers in the mills.   2. They
    worked very long days, were not paid overtime, and had no benefits.   3. Female workers
    had a hard time taking care of their children, and they were paid less than men.   4. She
    sadly told a story about a young girl who died in a mill accident.   5. They received warn-
    ings or lost their jobs.   6. Answers will vary.

Unit 10: Progress?

Interaction (page 60)

B. *General*   *Specific*
    2   15   1   9
    5   16   3   11
    8   17   4   13
    10 19   6   14
    12 20   7   18
C. 20 and 1;   2 and 13;   10 and 3;   19 and 4;   5 and 14;   17 and 6;   15 and 7;
    8 and 18;   12 and 9;   16 and 11

Reading Reaction (pages 62–64)

B. 1. T   3. F   5. T   7. T
    2. F   4. T   6. F   8. T
C. 1. food, weapons, and machinery   2. American movies, music, television, books, and
    computer software   3. Answers will vary.   4. They are in English; their treatment of
    American values.   5. Answers will vary.   6. the spread and invasion of another culture
    that undermines traditional values

Written Reaction (page 64)

A. 1. g   3. d   5. f   7. b
    2. c   4. h   6. a   8. e

Unit 11: Illegal Alien

Interaction (page 67)

B. 1. T   3. T   5. ?   7. ?
    2. T   4. T   6. F   8. F

Reading Reaction (pages 69–70)

B. 1. T   3. F   5. ?   7. F
    2. T   4. F   6. F   8. F

Pronunciation (page 72)

B. Acronyms pronounced like words: NATO, SCUBA, NASA, ASAP, AIDS, NAFTA,
    ROM, LASER

Written Reaction (page 73)

A. 2. h   4. f   6. e   8. a
   3. g   5. c   7. d

Unit 12: Energy Crisis

Interaction (page 75)

A. 1. f   3. d   5. e
   2. b   4. a   6. c

Reading Reaction (pages 77–78)

B. 1. petroleum and coal   2. Nuclear energy   3. gasoline, alcohol, and natural gas   4. wind, sun, and water   5. the sun   6. geothermal   7. The technology is not ready, and the costs are too high.   8. nuclear energy

Written Reaction (page 79)

A. 1. pollution   2. refinery   3. commute   4. elimination   5. to depend   6. to generate   7. to heat

Unit 13: Those Golden Years

Interaction (page 81)

B. 1. T   3. F   5. F   7. T
   2. F   4. F   6. T   8. F

C. 1. about 60 or 65   2. in a city   3. They don't think it's a good idea.   4. confused and excited   5. excited

Reading Reaction (pages 84–86)

B. 1. h   3. b   5. e   7. c
   2. g   4. f   6. d   8. a

C. 1. She lived longer than any other person on earth.   2. "Everything's fine."
   3. "It's nothing fixed; it's nothing absolute; it's nothing preset from the day you're born."
   4. Aging implies decay or decline in health. Growing older means living more years.
   5. stress, diet, exercise, and keeping busy   6. Stress is a factor in aging.   7. What we eat and how much is important. Even a little bit of exercise can help elderly people. Knowing how to deal with stress is important. Excessive smoking and drinking cause you to age faster. Keeping busy and feeling useful prevent aging.   8. Answers will vary.

Written Reaction (page 87)

A. 1. elderly   2. climate   3. to retire   4. physical   5. wrinkles   6. stress   7. aging

Unit 14: A Home for Little Sarah

Reading Reaction (pages 92–93)

B. 1. T   3. F   5. F
   2. T   4. T   6. F

C. 1. They feel adopting a black baby is simple.   2. Some social workers feel interracial adoption may be harmful.   3. She believes her parents gave her a wonderful home and a good education, and she feels grateful.   4. She feels that she has difficulty relating to other black people.   5. They understand.

Written Reaction (page 95)

A. 1. cultural heritage   2. identity crisis   3. low self-esteem   4. biological parent   5. adoptive parent

Unit 15: Life

Reading Reaction (pages 98–100)

B. *Incorrect Answers:*   1. terminally ill   2. a man   3. lives in a luxurious home, has a lot of clothes   4. a legal issue   5. supports assisted suicide   6. everywhere, in Michigan, for doctors

Written Reaction (page 102)

A. 1. f   3. b   5. d   7. e   9. c
    2. g   4. i   6. h   8. a

Unit 16: After-School Job

Interaction (pages 104–105)

B. 1. F   3. ?   5. T   7. F
    2. F   4. T   6. ?   8. F

Reading Reaction (pages 105–107)

B. 1. F   3. F   5. T   7. F
    2. F   4. ?   6. ?   8. T

C. 1. newspaper girl   2. She started driving her father's truck.   3. the dogs catching the papers, getting up very early, and having to pay for the window she broke
    4. Mrs. Thompson's kindness, making friends with Jethro, and the beauty of mornings
    5. Mrs. Thompson owned the fine, old house. The writer broke her window with a newspaper. Mrs. Wiley was the owner of the dog, Jethro.   6. Answers will vary.

Written Reaction (page 109)

A. 1. h   3. g   5. c   7. a
    2. f   4. e   6. d   8. b

Unit 17: Higher Education

Reading Reaction (pages 113–115)

B. 1. F   3. T   5. F   7. F
    2. T   4. T   6. F   8. F

C. 1. failing chemistry   2. drinks   3. a smoker, her husband   4. many windows, clean air
    5. she is pregnant, the baby will have her mother's name   6. he smokes, he drinks
    7. make her mother feel thankful, prepare her mother for bad news, ask for money
    8. doesn't exist

D. 1. He's younger than she is, works at a gas station, doesn't want to finish high school, has a learning disability, smokes two packs a day, and drinks too much and becomes violent.
    2. She's pregnant and drinks sometimes.   3. She lives in a small, one-room apartment where the air is not fresh, there is only one window, and she doesn't eat much.   4. She asks for money at the post office.   5. She is married and pregnant.   6. She is married to Todd, pregnant, and begs for money at the post office.   7. She needs to break the news that she's failing chemistry and to ask for money.   8. Answers will vary.

Written Reaction (page 115)

A. 1. f   3. h   5. e   7. c
    2. a   4. g   6. d   8. b

Unit 18: Peer Pressure

Reading Reaction (pages 119–120)

B. 1. F   3. ?   5. F   7. F
    2. F   4. F   6. ?   8. T

C. 1. A group of students at Columbine High School who dressed in black trench coats. 2. Their families were well off.   3. They were considered outsiders and strange. They dressed in black trench coats.   4. *Possible answer:* They wanted to kill popular students like athletes, those with high grades, and club leaders.   5. Twenty-five people were injured, and 15 people were killed.   6. Answers will vary.

Pronunciation (page 121)

d	*t*	*id*
occurred	dressed	wanted
realized	washed	started
injured	walked	collected
killed	danced	protected
used	searched	chatted
belonged	influenced	shouted
played	established	compensated
described	dropped	attempted
settled	watched	collected
learned	typed	
listened		

Written Reaction (page 122)

A. 1. f   3. e   5. c   7. d
    2. a   4. b   6. h   8. g

Unit 19: The Breadwinner

Interaction (pages 124–125)

B. 1. F   3. ?   5. F   7. F
    2. F   4. ?   6. F   8. ?

Reading Reaction (pages 125–127)

B. 1. T   3. F   5. T
    2. F   4. F   6. T

C. 1. less than half   2. divorce or because the parents decided not to marry   3. siblings (brothers, sisters, or brother and sister) who share only one common parent   4. Most single parents work to support their families. Some receive financial support from the other parent or from the government.   5. Some work because their income is needed. Some want to have a career.   6. More than half of American households are headed by a single parent, most by the mother, who needs to work to support her family. Also, the cost of living in many areas of the United States is high, so the mother's income of ten is needed to support the family, even in two-parent households.

Written Reaction (page 129)

A. 1. c   3. e   5. a   7. b
    2. f   4. g   6. d

Unit 20: On My Own

Interaction (pages 131–132)

C. 1. F   3. F   5. F   7. T
   2. F   4. T   6. ?   8. T

D. 1. He plans to share an apartment with his friend, Max.   2. his grandmother, and now his parents   3. They think he's too young.   4. He's moving out and into an apartment with Max, who is female.   5. his best friend   6. She thinks it's a good idea.   7. They're worried that he is too young to live by himself.   8. Answers will vary.

Reading Reaction (pages 132–133)

B. 1. F   3. ?   5. ?   7. T
   2. T   4. F   6. T   8. ?

C. 1. Al Codger   2. He feels negatively about them.   3. They look weird, smoke, drink, sometimes use foul language, and listen to rap music.   4. His grandson is one of them, and he's a good kid.

Written Reaction (pages 134–135)

A. 1. adolescence   2. club   3. criticize   4. disapprove   5. foul language   6. immature
   7. to share   8. upset